Praise for **MEANINGFUL MANIFESTATION**

"I couldn't be more thrilled about Alea Lovely's
Meaningful Manifestation. *Alea's IMAGINE method is pure
magic, guiding you through a deeply transformative journey
to manifest your true desires. Her wisdom and intuition shine
through every page, making this book a powerful tool for anyone
ready to live a more authentic and fulfilling life. Alea's gift for
creating real change is truly magical, and this book is
a testament to her incredible abilities."*

— ZOEY GRECO, intuitive empath and spiritual coach

*"Manifestation is so much more than wishing on a star. Alea
Lovely not only nails the intricacies of the manifestation process
with her IMAGINE method but explores the fullness of the
human experience along with it.* Meaningful Manifestation *is
a must-read for anyone looking to live their idea of a good life."*

— MEG BARTLETT, dream interpreter, oracle,
and galactic historian

Meaningful
MANIFESTATION

Meaningful MANIFESTATION

Imagination, Intuition, and Other Spiritual Sh*t

ALEA LOVELY

HAY HOUSE

HAY HOUSE LLC
Carlsbad, California • New York City
London • Sydney • New Delhi

Published in the United States by: Hay House LLC: www.hayhouse.com`*`
Published in Australia by: Hay House Australia Publishing Pty Ltd: www.hayhouse.com.au
Published in the United Kingdom by: Hay House UK Ltd: www.hayhouse.co.uk
Published in India by: Hay House Publishers (India) Pvt Ltd: www.hayhouse.co.in

Project editor: Sally Mason-Swaab
Cover design: Shubhani Sarkar • *Interior design:* Bryn Starr Best

Cataloging-in-Publication Data is on file at the Library of Congress

Tradepaper ISBN: 978-1-4019-7860-0
E-book ISBN: 978-1-4019-7861-7
Audiobook ISBN: 978-1-4019-7862-4

10 9 8 7 6 5 4 3 2 1
1st edition, November 2024

Printed in the United States of America

This product uses responsibly sourced papers and/or recycled materials. For more information, see www.hayhouse.com.

For Veda,
the light of my life.

CONTENTS

INTRODUCTION

What if I told you that manifestation as we know it could get you everything you thought you wanted and you still might not be happy? You would think I'm crazy, right? The million—maybe billion—dollar industry in coaching, workshops, conferences, books, and YouTube videos all teaching you how to attract that dream partner, get the house that you want, have the car and job that you want, get the life that you want . . . could possibly all be a lie.

A scary thought, but stick with me here.

Manifestation as we know it is brilliant as a concept, but why does it seem to work for so few people? Why are we not all millionaires, and why can't we just think positive enough to make those things happen for us?

After about 10 years of practicing the law of attraction, I've concluded that we all might be missing a key aspect of this "law." And if you're reading this, then I'm here to reveal to you findings that I hope will help you on your journey toward leading not just a good life but one that manifests what is meaningful to *you*.

What makes me qualified to take you on this journey? Well, let me tell you a story.

I have dreams. Like, big dreams of what I want to manifest in my life. My dreams are really important to me, but I also mean the dreams that come from going to bed at night and sleeping.

Since I was a kid, I would have dreams that would give me insight and inspiration about my life, and I started to get keen on paying attention to them. More than a few times, I would have dreams that would come true. Some of them predicted the death of a loved one, predicted when someone was pregnant, and even predicted major events that have happened around the world. Some of these dreams would be ancestors coming through with prophetic wisdom or messages for my family members, some were dreams where I astral traveled and learned from the Ancients in the Halls of Amenti, and some were dreams where my hands were crab claws and didn't make any fucking sense. I definitely have those too.

But within these dreams, there is a lot of crossover. Loads of manifestations have come to me in the dream world well before I experienced them in the physical. My partner came to me in a dream to tell me to wait for him four months before we met, my dream house (pun intended) came to me in a dream before I was even considering buying a home, and even my baby girl was announced to me in a dream 10 years before I even thought about having children.

These were some of my biggest dreams come true. These have brought incredible meaning to my life and helped me expand in ways I wouldn't have ever imagined. But there are still quite a few real physical dreams that I'd like to manifest. For instance, I would love to finally become a well-known (or at least well-paid) painter. And that my family and I could move to a foreign country and learn a language fluently or that my book would be on the *New York Times* bestseller list (here's to hoping!). I don't know where it comes from, but since I was a kid, I've always wanted these epic experiences. Even though I grew up really poor, there has always been something inside me that wanted more. Once

I have my mind set on something, it's kind of a done deal at that point. I was going to find a way to make that happen.

My mom taught us about manifestation before she even knew what that meant, but there was a phrase of hers that, to this day, I still think about. She said, "You are favored!" When we would be afraid that something wouldn't work out, she would say, "Act like you have favor!" When something would happen in our lives that didn't look possible but ended up happening, she would say "Favor!" in this singsongy, Oprah-esque exclamation. Here's an example of what I'm talking about.

I really wanted to get into this private school for college. They had the most beautiful campus and an attractive liberal arts curriculum. We didn't have private-school money, for one, but two, even though I had close to straight A's, I never tested well on the ACT. We didn't know I was dyslexic at the time, but for my brain standardized tests were just a fucking no-no. My mom prompted us to go to one of the school's inquiry days. It was my dream to go to that school, but I had no idea how I was going to get accepted and then actually pay for it.

While we were in the auditorium listening to the admissions counselors go on about grades, test scores, and scholarships, I started to feel anxious that this dream was never going to happen. And then I felt this very sharp sensation on the left side of my neck. I had been stung by a bee.

I started to feel really weird.

I quickly told my mom, and my mom yelled, "Help! She's been stung by a bee!" Suddenly all the attention was on me. It turns out I had an allergy I hadn't known about, so things got real alarming real quick. The counselors stopped what they were doing and quickly rushed to get me medical attention. I was sitting in their office with the dean himself pouring me a glass of water and making me an ice pack. They asked me if I needed food and wanted to monitor me to make sure my throat wouldn't close. They couldn't afford to have a student die on their property—it would be a PR mess.

While I was mortified that I had interrupted their entire presentation, my mom saw different circumstances. She said, "This is what's going to get you into this school. That bee was a sign. That was favor!" I rolled my eyes, because I didn't know how in the world me getting stung by a bee would be a favor. But she said, "Now everyone knows who you are. They will remember you when your application comes in; make the most of this!" And she was right. I sat in the office, talking with the admissions counselors about how much I wanted to go to this school. Two of them in particular took a liking to me and told me they would fight over my application and help me find scholarships I could apply for. And sure enough, I not only got into that school but also got enough scholarships to make it happen.

But there have been plenty of times where I didn't feel the "favor." Like from my mentally and emotionally abusive first marriage, or when rent was due and I didn't have enough to cover my bills, or when all my friends were getting married and having babies and I was the ugly duckling with no prospects, or when I wrecked my new car after only two months and tore all the cartilage away from my sternum for a lengthy recovery, or when my racist college professor repeatedly graded me and the other black students from our class extraordinarily low so we would lose our scholarships, or when I started to bleed out on the table during my C-section. Where was the favor then?

Many dreams didn't turn out like I thought they would, especially not in the timing *they were supposed to.* I had spent a lot of my life believing that I was unlucky.

What happens when manifesting doesn't work for you? Is it that what you're trying to manifest isn't meant for you? Or maybe we're manifesting the "wrong" way? Or is it that, just like the bee, all the things I just listed had their own lessons and happy endings when I was able to see it.

If you are reading this book and listen to the podcast *Spiritual Shit,* you might be already excited about what you're going to read here. You might know some of these stories and connect deeply with my message of Meaningful Manifestation. But if you found me perusing through an aisle in your local bookstore or online and have no idea who I am, buckle up. I'm going to take us in a somewhat different direction and maybe even a controversial way of thinking about manifestation that I hope helps you feel a little luckier and more favored in your day-to-day life.

Why did I write this book? Well, there are 10 million downloads on the podcast, so I kind of think it was because of you listeners. The episodes that got listened to the most were about manifestation. The podcast would always hit the number-one spot most frequently when I had episodes about manifestation. I think it's because we are all trying to figure out this game of life and how to get the best results possible. We all want to live a good life.

But the challenge is that the weight of our dreams is often so heavy, it can make us feel like we're drowning. There's so much we want to achieve in this short time on Earth, and sometimes the dreams we think we want are not even our own. We are pressured by our parents, society, friend groups, or even a wound . . . we need more to validate who we are and can never feel happy wading in one place.

Sometimes we clamor and thrash toward our dreams before we actually know how to swim, so we start to sink in stress and anxiety when it takes patience and training to get where we want to go. Sometimes our dreams bring out of us the depths of the ocean and expand us in incredible ways, but other times they can fall short because they bring out things that are very shallow and inauthentic. Sometimes life throws us in the deep end before we're ready, and we just need to wave our arms to keep our heads above water. Maybe you're in one of these stages right now.

Whatever stage you're in, I'm here to offer you a lifeline so you can swim gracefully through this life and not be afraid of your dreams, especially those that would make your life truly meaningful. You weren't put on this earth to "catch up" to everyone else, but you deserve to live a good life. *Your* good life.

Now, in this book, you won't be hearing any gaslighting about how you just need to think positive to get what you want because we aren't starting from the same place and don't swim at the same pace. We have to consider privilege, access, systemic oppression, societal "rules," trauma, and the like. Meaningful Manifestation requires us getting real about where we're starting from in relation to where we want to go whether favor plays a role, or not. And we will have to consider the possibility that what you're trying to manifest won't make you happy.

We have this happiness trap where we turn toward manifestation as the acquisition of things. More and more will make me happier. Except when it doesn't.

I had this insane six-month period of manifestation where I met my husband, got pregnant when doctors told me I was infertile, switched my dominant career of photography to my podcast and card readings, and bought a home during a tough housing market where the owner had higher offers and still chose us.

One night, around 3 A.M., I was having a particularly hard time breastfeeding. My 10-day-old infant was screaming at me for hours on end. I was in so much pain from my surgery, barely able to get in and out of bed on my own, and sitting in my beautiful home with my sleeping husband in the next room. He asked several times if he could help, but he very well couldn't sprout boobs right then and there, so I told him to go to sleep. I was exhausted; I couldn't properly feed my kid. My hormones were upside down, and I felt like I was failing. In that moment I felt the saddest I had ever felt. Wasn't all this supposed to make me happy?

Is this really what I wanted?

Why wasn't anyone speaking about what happens once you get all the things you've been trying to manifest and still don't feel complete? When you have the life that you dreamed about, and you still don't feel happy? Wasn't happiness the goal? I had everything around me that I could have ever wanted for years on end. But not the happily ever after. I manifested like a boss and yet . . . why didn't I feel any relief? Why didn't I feel any favor?

And so, this is the beginning of a new story, the one I'll tell in the pages of this book. I had come to another inflection point. One where I have turned upside down the happiness trap and what it means to live a good life. A truly meaningful existence on your own terms. What I came to understand, and what I'll outline in the upcoming chapters, is that if you can't find purpose, fulfillment, and meaning in your life, none of the other things you manifest will matter.

I had practiced my manifestation beliefs for a long time, but it wasn't rooted in my core beliefs. In fact, I hadn't yet determined my core beliefs. That absence led to unrealistic expectations about manifestation, and the expectations themselves were the cause of my suffering. This idea that happiness came out of a bigger and better thing. But I had missed the aspects of gratitude and depth to enjoy what I manifested thus far. More importantly, manifestation is not an end point or a way to free ourselves from discomfort. We're alive on this earth, and that will always mean a certain amount of discomfort. But we can immerse ourselves and find joy in Meaningful Manifestation, a never-ending process of evolving and expanding, finding out more about who we are and why we are here.

It was at that desperate middle-of-the-night moment that I began the journey that helped me understand just how complex manifestation is. It is not about getting. It is about healing. Transformation. And growth.

In the pages ahead, trust that I'm not going to give formulas for how to manifest an even bigger yacht. That's not the vibe, y'all. I will instead address the gaps that other manifestation books may skip over. Why did manifesting get to be such a big deal anyway? Because it told us that we have the power to change our destiny. It said that we aren't a victim of circumstances and that we can be empowered to make substantial changes in our life. But what it didn't mention is that sometimes we encounter different and even extraordinary challenges with the chance to grow, and growth feels, at times, deeply uncomfortable. Growth and discomfort are a part of manifestation. So, a perspective shift is needed.

We are talking about manifesting a perspective on life, that whatever you are going through, you will find your path. The stories and advice are real, they're raw, and I believe they are going to change your life. I will share my IMAGINE method, the manifestation framework that I have been working on and perfecting, taking in all I learned before my 3 A.M. revelation and all the relevant knowledge I've acquired since.

Meaningful Manifestation will give you a complete roadmap to create a magical life that is full of meaning. Following my IMAGINE method, we'll bring more joy, abundance, and purpose into your life. What does IMAGINE stand for? Glad you asked. The IMAGINE method will guide you through the following seven steps:

I is for Inception: Where are you starting?

M is for Manifestation: What do you want?

A is for Anti-Belief: What is the belief challenging what you want?

G is for Growth: What change needs to happen to get what you want?

I is for Integration: How do you apply that change to your life?

N is for Notice: Observing the signs and syncs to help you produce more of it.

E is for Expansion: What do you do once you have realized your manifestation?

By opening the pages of this book, you are stepping across a powerful threshold, inviting change, growth, and transformation into your life. I'm ready to take this journey with you, guided by *your* voice, *your* values, *your* experiences, and *your* dreams. What will you call in to your life? What questions will you ask? What new stories will you tell? What magic will you bring forth into the world? The magic already exists inside you. Let's find out how you'll use it to transform your life. Who will you become?

Let's find out.

Chapter 1

The Philosophy of a Good Life

Once the spiritual world opened up to me—or perhaps I should say once I opened up to it—I started to think a lot about big life questions. I thought about them with every cell of my body. On my podcast and in my research, I contemplated the universe, the past, and the meaning of life. Questions beget more questions. *Why are we here? Where did we come from? Are loved ones sending us messages from the other side? What is the other side? What do our dreams mean? What is the universe trying to tell us? In short, what is the point of this life?*

At the same time, I was immersing myself in the practice of manifestation, but the closer I got to the things that I wanted to call into my life, the more I began to realize that there was no endpoint. When would it start to feel like enough? When would I feel like I had what I desired? Despite having manifested the most beautiful things I could have imagined, I wasn't fully happy. The things that I had built up as the answers to my happiness didn't get me the desired feelings once I had them. It became this game of acquiring more and more until I was standing in the middle of everything, questioning what I wanted in the first place.

I had followed a traditional method of manifestation, and that meant my focus had been on what was lacking, missing, or needed to be fixed. In other words, on all the things I still didn't have. Meanwhile, the intense amount of attention spent grasping for bigger and better was sucking all the beauty and magic out of the new life I'd created for myself. When does the search for bigger and better stop? Isn't there always something "bigger" and "better" out there? All it does is make everything you have feel like it's not enough. I knew this focus on what is lacking, missing, or broken was not the kind of manifestation path I wanted to pursue.

So, on the one hand, I was knee deep in abstract questions about life "out there," in some realm far beyond our daily lives; and on the other, I was caught in the endless cycle of acquiring thing after thing, experience after experience, without feeling like I was able to enjoy my own days.

Always teaching me, life intervened yet again. In 2022, my aunt died unexpectedly. She was in her mid-50s. Among my mom's seven siblings, my mom was closest to her—we had grown up playing with her kids. My aunt had been through a lot in her life, and now it was suddenly over. Sidenote: I don't deal with death very well. I think it's what motivated me to do mediumship work because I have such a high level of discomfort with death. I have both a fascination and a terror with the aspect of a soul leaving this earth and what it means for the life that they left. It's one of the existential things that I ruminate about the most: Why are we here?

After my aunt passed, I couldn't stop thinking about her—the choices and the sacrifices she'd made. The questions that I continued to ruminate on were: Did she live a good life? And what exactly is a good life? Exploring abstract spiritual questions had gotten me far, but it had also taken me far away from thinking about what makes the days meaningful to me. Yet immersing myself in manifestation the way I understood it at the time led me to the emptiness of always wanting something out of reach. This sudden loss brought what was important and meaningful to me in focus.

My aunt's death made it clear I needed to pivot once again. We all thought she had more time . . . that we had more time with her. And it just hit me, suddenly, how often we take our loved ones for granted, how often we take the time we have for granted.

We have such a limited time here on earth, and we never know when it might suddenly end, so we better figure out what it means to live a good life while we're here. Of course we can continue to debate bigger spiritual questions. (Trust me, I'm not giving up on those anytime soon.) But in the meantime, I needed to turn my thinking from the things I still didn't have or understand to thinking about the *kind* of life I wanted to lead.

Seizing this idea—that we need to aim for a good life rather than grasp for thing after thing from a manifestation to-do list—changed my approach to manifestation entirely. This is where it started to get really *meaningful*! I went from desperately pursuing one goal after another to building a clear vision of what a good life means to me and eventually to creating the IMAGINE method I briefly described in the introduction. Just to give you a quick recap, each letter stands for an essential part of the overall approach.

Inception: Where are you starting?

Manifestation: What do you want?

Anti-Belief: What is the belief challenging what you want?

Growth: What change needs to happen to get what you want?

Integration: How do you apply that change to your life?

Notice: Observing the signs and syncs to help you produce more of it.

Expansion: What do you do once you have realized your manifestation?

I'll take these steps one by one in the chapters that follow. What it comes down to is perspective.

We can change our reality by changing our perspective. And I don't mean this in the sense of you will finally get the things you want by being more positive. What I mean is that you can start to love what you have by shifting your focus on what is meaningful to you. That happiness isn't brought on by the new house, the car, the partner, the career, and so on. Realizing that a good life, in fact, comes down to just a few nonnegotiables that make us feel fulfilled on a deeper level.

Finally internalizing this concept felt like *magic*. It was like I was seeing my life with new eyes. I loved the idea that I could be happier with less or even just focusing more deeply on what mattered overall. With society's capitalistic influence of more is more, the pursuit of happiness had made me feel empty, like I was in a trap. It felt like I was running after someone else's version of what was supposed to make me happy, and time after time, I was disappointed that it didn't give me the feeling I was searching for. The pursuit itself had to change.

Magic.

Who doesn't love magic? Creating something out of nothing. Bending the rules of nature. Transcending our limitations. So much magic already exists around us, but we're intent on rushing ahead with our goals for that day or that week. In that rush, we're missing out on the magic that's there. We have let it become normal and even mundane to us. People think it's pretty magical to call into our

4

lives something we have been hoping for, but this pivot for me meant that magic wasn't any longer about manifestation but instead about observing life. I understood that the mundane could be magical if we had the eyes to see it. I was taking magic off the pedestal, always looking for something epic and bringing it down to earth.

For most of us, magic is a mysterious concept that we only dream of experiencing. It's another elusive idea "out there" that we see in romantic movies or glimpse in childhood memories. But what if we experience magic all the time and just haven't trained our eyes to see it?

As children, we saw it all the time, and easily: in a night swim, a new friend, and a walk through the forest on an afternoon in autumn. Now, it's even looking at the child I made and being able to feed her from my body at 3 A.M. As we grow older, we tend to lose the sense of wonder and magic that we had so easily as children. We stop seeing the extraordinary in the ordinary. The responsibilities and demands of adult life consume us, leaving little time or energy to appreciate the simple pleasures and beauty that surround us. We become so focused on achieving our goals and fulfilling our obligations that we forget to pause and take in the wonder of the world.

The same thing happens with the practice of manifestation, which we've been told is supposed to be like magic for us. We become so caught in the process of acquisition that it becomes an endless search, often feeling stressful and forced. Chasing after "better," we lose sight of what makes us feel good or gives us fulfillment. We lose sight of the values in the kind of life we're trying to manifest.

For example, imagine that you are scrolling through Zillow looking at houses you cannot yet afford (a favorite pastime of mine). And in seeing these wonderful spaces, you start to find discontent in your own home. Or maybe it's a scroll session on Pinterest, where you see incredible inspiration for what you want to do in your home, or your favorite home influencer just renovated their bathroom and your ideas are spinning. None of these things are inherently wrong; however, now you're looking at your home in a not-so-favorable light. You start to think that this place you have isn't good enough, and the discontent begins to flood your everyday and increase your annoyances with what you don't yet have. Ever experienced that?

Imagine that you realize you are one of the few people actually able to buy a home in the last five years. People your age are drowning in rent prices, and you happened to have enough ducks in a row to buy the house you are pooh-poohing right now. Imagine serving at a soup kitchen, where a few hundred unhoused folks are without shelter. How do you feel about your house now? Suddenly, that outdated kitchen is a functional space where your family creates memories and eats the abundance of food that you are able to buy every week. Suddenly, you are very thankful for that outdated home with the memories you get to create in it, and *that,* my friend, is where the magic begins to show itself.

I'll give you another example. At the time of writing this book, I'm not working a ton. My husband and I are working around a schedule that allows us to be with our toddler full time between the two of us. It's been tough for me not to have autonomy over my time and not be able to make as much money as I know that I'm capable of making. Money has always signified freedom to me after growing up really poor: the choice to do what I want, when I want, without having to ask for permission. Cutting my work hours in half meant not traveling like I want to this year, or scaling down on the birthday parties we have for our kids, or putting away more in savings to make sure we have enough for a surprise expense. It requires a great deal more of planning and responsibility, and it means that five days a week, my job is raising a rambunctious toddler while squeezing work in during naptimes, late evenings, and even 5 A.M. sessions before sunrise. It has meant that my business isn't as successful as I would like it to be, and a part of myself is fighting with those feelings of autonomy I once had.

But in the throes of those tough feelings, I realized, wow, how fortunate we are to be able to see my daughter grow up in these formative years. How wonderful that I get to be the one who raises her, that I get the privilege of shaping this young child's experiences, and I get to be her protector. I have just a couple more years before she's in school full time and how short and beautiful this season with her is. Every new thing she discovers is a possibility for me to see things anew through her eyes. One of my favorite videos I have is her sharing sheer excitement at me blowing a dandelion at her for the first time. I could listen to the awe in her voice for hours because it is literally pure magic! Yes, I could bemoan us having less money and that my job these days had become more about washing dishes and changing diapers than hitting number one on the podcast charts again. But that would mean possibly missing the magic my daughter has been sent here to help me see.

Losing the ability to see the magic in our lives doesn't mean it's not there. I hope that in the pages of this book, you'll find that it's still all around us, waiting for us to rediscover it. Everyday magic (or magic in the everyday) is a part of the good life. And living a good life means departing from many of the messages we are getting about what we need to be happy. We can start by learning to appreciate what we have and where we are right now.

I'll give you another quick example. I've lived in Kansas City most of my life, and sometimes I really want to get the hell out of here. "We have to move," I often find myself telling my husband. But of course we can't move because of our blended family, and sometimes the itch is so strong that we've even talked to the kids' mom about whether she'd be willing to move.

At a friend's wedding in Sedona last summer, I was struck by the gorgeous mountain landscape and the beautiful weather. What would it be like to live in the desert? If I lived there, I'd be hiking and way more active because of the outdoors. Kansas City is a sedentary life where you drive even if it's only a few blocks. In New York, I'd walk 20 blocks without blinking. What about Chicago? I could see us moving to Chicago. I started to imagine what life in the Windy City would be like. It has many of the advantages of New York that I had before. But I definitely couldn't deal with at least two months of winter. Winters there are absurd! So, we'd have to do something like go to Mexico for January and February. But we could go to Mexico in the winter now, without the added stress and cost of living in Chicago.

Where else could we move? Europe? Europe is lovely. We're not in a stage where we could do that yet. But if not Europe or another country—which we can't feasibly do— then do we really need to move?

When I got back from Sedona, I looked around, and it was clear I had literally everything I needed right there in Kansas City, where I started. And nearly everything I wanted for this season of my life. My family and friends are here. We have community in our neighborhood where our kids can play with each other. The cost of living isn't nearly as crazy here as it is everywhere else. We have a thriving art community and lots of interesting events and people. Our sports teams are winning back-to-back titles, and we are never short of good coffee, beer, and barbecue. (If you're from Texas, I'm sorry, but KC BBQ is better. Fight me.) The summers are not great; they're humid. The winters are cold. But if we can make enough money, we can take trips to enjoy beautiful weather and the ocean. Plus, for our beautiful home, we're paying half what my friends pay for their apartments in any other city.

In the end, I circle back to realizing I'm not appreciating what I have: a decent cost of living, a community that cares about my family, and day-to-day overall ease when it comes to the logistics of daily living. I remember when I moved back from New York to KC and needed to get an apartment. The process for an apartment in New York might have been the craziest thing I have ever experienced. One apartment asked me for $40k upfront to move in, plus background checks, credit checks, and then a letter so they would pick who they'd like to have in the building. It was worse than a job application process. They would ask for a promissory note on keeping your first-born child as rent collateral if they could. When I moved back to KC, I was shocked that I could put down $200 and give a signature to rent an apartment with no credit check because "you seem like a good candidate" seemingly based on intuition? I wasn't questioning it; I was just happy to have a place to live.

A lot of the fantasizing I do comes from being burned out. So, the problem may not be the location as much as the lifestyle that leads to the burnout. I could spend energy manifesting a move to some other city, which will come with all its own problems. Or I could spend that energy creating a life where we can take trips to actually *enjoy* the mountains or the ocean.

This story is kind of comical, and it's just a little anecdote to illustrate what I mean about appreciating what you have. The process of Meaningful Manifestation will take a bit longer than a daydream on a hike in Arizona. Still, it can point us in the direction of what I mean by Meaningful Manifestation. Since we know the path of wanting and acquiring more and more is not the manifestation we're looking for, let's get clear on what manifestation really is. Then we can move toward defining our Maxims and start bringing our lives into alignment with our philosophy of a good life.

And, weirdly, paradoxically, this manifestation process will lead us to start appreciating more of what we have. It will help usher in an acceptance of what is, the more we are able to come into the present of what a good life really means for each of us and what that good life looks like. But to some, a good life may not feel like it's always accessible.

The present can be fraught. It is not always filled with peace. In fact, as I was writing this book, violence erupted in the Middle East, and the impact reverberated around the world. Here, I am hoping to guide you toward a good life, whatever that looks like for you, while unimaginable numbers of people are losing their lives, and hatefulness seems to be exploding from every direction.

It is a luxury to manifest the life we want and to love the life we have. Many positive people full of gratitude and good intentions are living terrible circumstances that are not their fault at all. If you have the opportunity to even think about these concepts and what makes a good life for yourself, then your basic needs are being met and you are not most likely fighting for your survival in a war zone.

It's an incredible privilege to think about manifesting the lives we want and appreciating the lives we have. At times, that privilege has made me feel conflicted. Many days during this past fall, I was consumed with something like guilt. Seeing lives torn apart in Gaza, Sudan, Congo,

Ukraine, and many more, it's hard not to wonder why them and not me? Why are those mothers burying their children, and we're tucking ours into cozy beds at night?

Social media feeds update us continuously on the horrors overseas and sometimes in our own backyard, so we are inundated with images of trauma. It makes us feel like shit, honestly. And yet even deciding to take a *break* from the news is a privilege. To say, "You know what? I need to go for a walk." Or "I'm going to take a bath. I have to clear my energy." "I'm going to focus on a good life." We didn't even choose to live where we are, yet it gives us the privilege of looking away, and that can come with immense guilt.

Feeling outraged and guilty, spending time debating, and feeling divided—all that takes away from our energy to help. No one is ever truly awake when caught in these guilt cycles. To show up, to contribute, to be intentional about our attention, those are the spaces from where we can empower ourselves enough to contribute in a positive way.

When I came into this awareness, my focus shifted a bit. I feel guilt sometimes, but I know that's a trap, and it doesn't do shit. Mostly, I feel gratitude—immense gratitude. When I lay my daughter down at night, I feel so fortunate. I didn't choose to be born here, and those mothers didn't choose to be born there. Guilt doesn't help, but gratitude, recognizing my privilege, brings me to a place where I can help others, where I can hold love and empathy. I'm 10 times more likely to step up and do something about the injustice I see in the world when I'm in a space of gratitude than when I'm feeling down or avoidant about what happens in the world. And it brings more meaning to my life to know that I have the chance to help others when I can act on it. Humans are hardwired for connection, and helping others often gives us an immense boost toward finding lasting meaning in our lives. If I know that I made someone else's day better or even life better, man, that feels so much better than getting a new car.

Aiming to lead a good life is indeed a worthy aim. For me, a good life means not carrying hate for other people. A good life means one lived in love. This perspective offers humility. Not that our desires should be villainized, but, dear, we do have a lot to be grateful for, don't we? Recognizing that allows me to give more through activism and charity work. I can imagine that I feel nothing I have is good enough, or my heart doesn't have the capacity to give anything, but when I feel gratitude, I can help others from a place of fullness and love, not from guilt, fear, or anger. We have to cultivate empathy and hold on to it.

I think a good life has to do with helping others. Rejecting hopelessness and helplessness, allowing in gratitude and love—this is how I'll make good on my Maxims, my values. Living in harmony with others.

To live a good life, you have to know yourself. The question is, what makes a good life *for you*? This book encourages you to be curious about that. It's about finding out what matters to you. Sometimes I worry that people are over the idea of manifestation. Maybe they've tried it and found it didn't work. They've chanted, they've called in good things, thought positively, and looked for signs, but they can't afford their monthly rent. Maybe they got sold into the matrix of consumerism, the idea that bigger is better and the endless rope of pulling that just ends up in a fatigued match of tug-of-war.

I wonder if together we can re-enchant ourselves with manifestation, coming at it from a new way: that manifestation isn't about consuming more but living more, feeling more. That the magic we seek comes in the nuance and the ordinary of our human lives. As we practice, we can allow ourselves to grapple with world and life events that make it hard at times to even put our overwhelming feelings into words, let alone know what we truly want.

I suspect somewhere there's a voice inside you that *does* know what you want. It has a pretty good handle on what makes a good life for you. Introspection will be at the heart of our manifestation process. For that reason, I hope you like questions as much as I do.

Chapter 2

What Is Manifestation . . . Really?

*A lot of people will say my life is magic,
and I love that word, but it is confusing because
it's not magic—it's a choice to see it.*

— BETHANY SIMONS

Sometime in my early 20s, I let go of my religion. I had been Christian for a long time, but I couldn't stomach some of the basic tenets, like the idea that people should go to hell because they did not believe the same things someone else did. Whatever believing meant, it had to be bigger than that, more hopeful and expansive. Believing had to be about opening up possibilities, not shutting them down.

For a while I felt like I had nothing to hold on to. I no longer had the anchor of going to church. I no longer prayed. I'd left everything to move to London for a relationship that had failed. When I landed back in Kansas City, my house was in shambles. (I had let my brother and his friends rent it, and they hadn't taken care of it. It was no longer livable.) I didn't have a job. I didn't have any money coming in. I had two friends who let me crash with them, but I didn't like the feeling of having to rely on someone else. What was I doing? Where was I going? I needed something to pull me out of the funk I'd fallen into. Something that could center me.

I was lying in a twin bed, looking up at the ceiling in my friend's guest room, thinking about all I had given up living in London only to come back with nothing. I took a major risk, and to my 25-year-old sensibilities, it felt like I had nothing to show for it.

Somehow, I put one foot in front of the other and got myself to the gym. I was on the treadmill scrolling YouTube when a video about manifestation caught my eye. This was before manifestation was even a word that we were using in our daily vernacular. It was Rhonda Byrne's short documentary, *The Secret*. "What is the law of attraction?" All these successful people were talking about how you can imagine something, ask for something, and it would come into your life.

After my world had felt like it had crashed down around me, this sprung me into a moment of hope. It cracked my cloud of depression and gave me the chance to see my future with new eyes.

I got my hands on the full movie of *The Secret* and ran to Barnes & Noble to buy the book and anything else I could binge on the Law of Attraction. I watched the documentary every day, to the point where I almost had it memorized. The voices of its philosophers, visionaries, and quantum physicists were the soundtrack to my life during that era. It was like a gateway drug into spirituality and mysticism.

I was a photographer at the time, and I had moved back to Kansas City from London in late spring, after most people in Kansas City had booked their photographers for their summer weddings. I was broke. But *The Secret* gave me hope. It was clear that there was work. I just needed to book it in a different time frame, an earlier time frame like early spring. That realization gave me hope that I could get out of living at my friend's house and move back into my own!

I set the goal that I would book five weddings, and in one week I booked seven. "It fucking works!" I was elated that all this positive thinking had changed my circumstances majorly. It was exciting to gain this new awareness around how thought could direct my life. By thinking about something I wanted, I could bring it into my life. I was at the start of a new way of living. A new way of understanding the universe, even. A fledgling power.

I could change my circumstances with my thoughts. It felt simultaneously radical and familiar. Time is not linear, so perhaps this is not surprising. As a child, I'd been taught, through prayer, that our thoughts can change what happens to us. This new understanding was, in a sense, a circling back to the person I had once been.

But as I've learned more about manifestation through my own research and by interviewing spiritual experts on my podcast, I've come to understand that the Law of Attraction isn't really a law. Or at least it doesn't operate like most of our laws. Laws are things that will happen the same way every time. Some practitioners will tell you manifestation works the same way every time, like a law, but that's not true. It's far more complex than that.

Let's consider the Law of Universal Gravitation. Anytime and anywhere, if you jump off the top of the stairs, you are going to plunge quickly toward the floor. You can take your experiment over to the other side of the world, you can get someone who is a billionaire to jump off the top of the stairs, or you can do it while Mercury is in retrograde, and the same thing is going to happen. The jump will be followed by a quick plunge to the floor. It doesn't discriminate, and it doesn't care about your privilege, how much money you make, or what country you live in. It doesn't care about your skin color or starting point or health. You could jump off the Empire State Building or the Eiffel Tower, and in all these scenarios, you will be subjected to the law of gravitational pull. Gravity won't care that you have 2 million followers.

That's not what we're talking about when we talk about manifestation, so I don't think *law* is the right word to use. I think it makes more sense to me to call it a principle because it feels a bit like gaslighting to say that no matter how it works, it works the same for everyone, right? The people in war-torn countries having their homes blown to pieces just didn't think positively enough, eh? Blacks marching in Selma for equal rights didn't believe hard enough that they were equal, huh? The queer people hiding in the bathroom from an active shooter just didn't have their thoughts in full alignment, hmm?

Hate to be so raw but that is the truth, right? If it's a law, then it would have to work every time and the same for everyone, and it simply does not. It doesn't mean that this principle is a throwaway because it has immense value to our perspective and how we can draw changes in our lives based on the lessons we might want to learn. But I had to put that here so you understand that sometimes it isn't that you suck at manifestation. Sometimes it's timing, and sometimes it's oppressive systems in place that cause systemic consequences for those who didn't create those structures.

Manifestation doesn't work the same way for each person, all the time, every time.

I've also come to understand that what I'm interested in pursuing is deep, *authentic* needs. A lot of times when we talk about manifestation, the focus is on materialistic things: how to win the lottery or bring in a fancy beach vacation that we can brag about to our friends. Manifestation becomes a kind of aimless browsing through the catalog of the universe, where we put energy toward what we think we should have to feel happy and complete. It becomes an endless cycle of acquiring thing after thing, gathering things just for the sake of having them, but maybe more so to show to others that we are worthy. At times we want these measures of success to validate us, and it usually leaves us feeling empty, no matter how big the pile of things.

Got that Chanel bag.

Now what?

The giant penthouse in the city.

Awesome. A pile of clothes. Closets full of shoes. The prettiest furniture . . . okay, what next?

Chasing something, but what?

This cycle is energetically heavy. It keeps us feeling trapped.

What intrigues me is Meaningful Manifestation—bringing forward traits within ourselves that will facilitate our growth and healing. When we manifest something we want into our life, if it's meaningful, then it changes us and helps move us a little further along into the people we want to become. The constant need for just acquiring stuff masks who we are at the core and instead hyperfocuses on what people see that can validate our existence. We use things as status, leverage, and proof that we are worthy of being seen, even being loved. We become so focused on managing all the stuff that those layers can sometimes cloud who we are at our core.

Manifestation acts as an alchemic tool that aids and sparks an understanding of our power. It is the practical aspects of our life meeting the magical outcomes we perhaps didn't know were possible. It's the frequency we most align with that helps us attract the magical experience our soul desires.

I know all this sounds a bit complex. As we continue over the course of the book, we'll keep spiraling back to these ideas, and they will start to become clearer, especially because you'll be immersed in your own process of manifesting growth and healing. You'll have aha moments along the way where you feel that frequency and alignment, and yes, even magic.

For now, think of it like this:

Manifestation is a perspective shift.

Manifestation is becoming a better vibrational match to the things you *truly* want.

Manifestation helps you fall in love with the life you already have.

Manifestation is about well-being.

Feel rather than act.

Know you have power inside you.

Energetic flow.

Tap into spirit.

Understand your own energy and what it can bring into your life.

Seek and find a vibrational match.

Get out of the space of limitation.

Change your pattern.

Know you came into this life to learn.

Make a conscious choice to be present.

Let go of the need to know *when* your manifestation will come.

Let your authentic desire be known.

Ask from a different place.

Get out of your own way.

Surrender.

Know you are worthy.

Listen to your body.

Call in patience. (Or, welcoming an opportunity for patience.)

Be ready to make intense changes.

Sharpen your intuition.

Attune yourself to a shift in energy.

Think about the root of what you want to manifest.

Ask: What is the feeling you think that will give you?

Let yourself experiment with what your manifestation might look like. Use a Pinterest board. Use a mood board. Try an online search. Flip through magazines. Imagine it. See it in the next form.

Deepen your relationship with yourself.

Know that you know the answer.

Accept the mysteries of the liminal space that we are in.

Evolve.

Believe it is okay to take care of yourself.

Absolve yourself of pressure to make something happen.

Open up your spirit.

Be bold enough to ask.

Do not push against time.

Do not push against anything.

Manifest a new perspective.

Ask yourself why you want something.

Do not compare yourself to someone else's timeline.

Know you are perfect as you are.

Trust yourself.

Remove energetic resistance.

Ask the right questions.

Become the author of your own story.

Overcome imprints.

Imagine Magic.

By accepting the call to this adventure of turning thought into fruition, you'll come to better understand yourself and what's important to you: what matters, not just asking what's next.

Manifesting what is meaningful will make what you actually want so clear you will never again find yourself running after things you "think" will make you happy. Instead, you will pursue desires that stem from the heart.

In the next chapter, Determine Your Maxims for a Good Life, we will learn whether the things we desire are authentic, innate to us, or something imposed on us from the outside world, what I call an inauthentic desire. During the interviews I hosted for my show *Spiritual Shit*, one topic that came up repeatedly is that people have been trained not to trust themselves. Their intuition has taken a backseat to the anxieties the modern world is foisting upon them.

When we're not truly connected to ourselves, it's hard to know what we really want and what will make us happy. Our world is dealing with an unhappiness epidemic because we are being taught that the wrong things matter. We need a framework to come back to ourselves, understand ourselves, and realize that it doesn't take a yacht and a million followers to be happy and have a good life. Rather, it takes courage to work out what we really want and then ask for it.

Most of the time, the desires that we have, the things that truly pull at our hearts, are things that we're meant to have in this lifetime. But manifestation is also seasonal. In the pages ahead, we'll talk about how our timeline might not always align with that of the universe and how, perhaps above all else, manifestation teaches us patience and vulnerability. To receive, we must open ourselves up to what the universe has in store for us.

Chapter 3

Determine Your Maxims for a Good Life

Going to the gym has never been my favorite activity. For many years, I've had an unhealthy relationship with exercise. As an athlete in school, I pushed my body to the limit running track and having 40-something men tell me I would be faster if I lost weight. I only started running track in the seventh grade because I thought I was fat. I started skipping meals and exercising close to four hours a day, and for almost two decades, I hadn't given my body the nutrients it needs. As a result, my body lost trust in me. My hormones were so severely unregulated that when I finally chose to eat healthy and stop working out like mad, it was too late. The damage had been done.

One morning in August, I was up really early. It was something like 5:30 A.M. as I begrudgingly walked like a zombie trying to muster up the courage not to quit my workout because I'd had a health scare a few weeks prior that shook me up pretty badly. On the treadmill, I was reliving my daughter holding my hand in the emergency room while I was feeling my heart jump around in ways it's not supposed to and feeling so scared that I would exit my body and leave her without a mom. While I was walking this morning in August, a message came to me.

If anything happens to you, your daughter won't have a mom. She needs you.

The voice continued.

You need to do everything you can to stay here as long as you possibly can.

When you were pregnant, you would have done anything to keep her alive and make sure she was taken care of. Now that she's outside of you, you're not doing everything you can to make sure she's taken care of . . . By taking care of yourself, you are taking care of her.

It was true. The message got to me in a big way because I would do *anything* to keep my family safe and give them what they need, but I wouldn't do the same for myself. In my world, I was used to putting myself last. During pregnancy, I had done everything in my power to make sure my daughter and I were safe. I took my supplements, I walked, I kept to a low-glycemic diet, and I went to the doctor every single week and checked my blood pressure every morning. I was losing weight during pregnancy because I was such a compliant patient, doing exactly what the doctors asked me to do to avoid insulin shots, and when that didn't work, I painfully injected myself every day to make sure my body could be a safe passage to carry her into this world. But this message I was getting on the treadmill made it clear that I had dropped the ball, not because I wasn't being a good mom but because I wasn't being a good steward of myself, and I guess spirit knew that if I wouldn't do it for myself, I would definitely do it for her.

I couldn't argue with the logic of the message I was receiving. I was working insane hours. I wasn't eating right, I wasn't taking all my supplements, and I wasn't being as active as I wanted because I have this neural pathway so ingrained that once I decide I'm going to be "healthy" (which was always equated to skinny in my generation), a trigger would go off in my brain that I was going to basically kill myself to get there.

It was undebatable. Since my daughter is my priority, my *health* has to be a priority as well. Taking care of myself has to be one of my Maxims for a Good Life.

Have you ever had a moment of clarity like that? A moment where the distractions of the day disappear, and everything comes into sharp focus?

This is what matters for me to live a good life.

Don't worry if you haven't. As you've probably figured out by now, I get a lot of messages. Spirit does a good job of being able to speak through me, and I try to be open to that voice as a channel.

But you don't have to figure out what matters in a moment of epiphany. Sometimes it's a process, and sometimes it's blatantly obvious. My health is one of my Maxims for a Good Life, but the others I figured out through a slightly more involved process. Together, we can use that process to help figure out what matters most to you. Before we get to candles, quiet music, meditation, affirmations, or vision boards, we need to know what you want at the center of your life. What is most meaningful to you? This chapter is an invitation to self-reflection. It's a time for spaciousness. For clarity. For deep intention and authenticity. And, as we'll see, it's a time to allow for the vulnerability that makes space for that epiphany and thus the transformation.

In the last chapter, we talked about what manifestation really is. We know it's not about acquiring things or chasing after a forever-out-of-reach idea of perfection. Manifestation is about creating and appreciating a good life that might be right in front of you. It's about finding the magic already inside you. It's about arriving at a point where every now and then, in the midst of the chaos, you can take a deep breath and be in your now and know it's where you want to be.

Let's start with brainstorming about what, for you, makes a good life. What would make you feel that you could take a breath once in a while and know that despite the never-ending to-do list and the daily frustrations and even really challenging obstacles, you are living the life you want to live?

Think big. Take out markers or open a mind-mapping app on your phone or laptop. Pull back the lens from the everyday minutia and think about times when you feel truly fulfilled. What kinds of things give you that feeling? When do you feel present and connected? What is most important to you? What do you value? If you got to the end of your life, what would you think over the years made a good life?

We can get at these Maxims from different angles. One of these questions might spark 10 pages of free writing. Others could leave you uninspired. So, feel free to try one, and if nothing comes, ignore it, and go on to something else. It might also help to carry a small journal with you so you can jot down notes as they come to you throughout your day.

Here are a few more prompts. Take as long as you like to work through them. Maybe hole yourself up in the library stacks on a rainy day and let yourself write and dream for hours. Or write about them while you are on the toilet and your toddler isn't giving you any privacy. Choose your fancy.

What do you care about most in life?

What kind of person do you want to be?

What kind of impact do you want to have on the world around you?

What do you want people to remember about you?

At the end of your life, when you look back, what will make you feel like you have no regrets?

As a medium contacting those who have passed, I have spent a lot of time dwelling on this last question. When mediumship was my main focus, I would connect with someone who had chosen to end his or her life at least once a day. That experience sent me into researching end-of-life studies. Looking back, what would people do differently if they could? How would they refine their priorities? Again and again, on their deathbeds, people said they wished they had led a more authentic life, living by their own rules. That struck a chord with me. How often are we living our lives according to what someone else wants for us or what we think society expects? You owe no one for being born on this chaotic ball hurtling through space, so why conform to a box that keeps you from being free?

Are you living by your own rules? You and I both still have time to make new ones up and start living our lives by them. This is an opportunity to figure out what those rules are. What are our nonnegotiables?

These will become our Maxims for a Good Life.

Look back over what you wrote in response to the questions above. Add or cross out anything you want. These responses are the raw material that will help us generate a list of what matters most. (Spoiler: You can create your Maxim list and make it official and still change it as many times as you want throughout your life, so don't overthink it.) Now if you're like me, you didn't write those all out, and you are speed reading ahead to see what other things I'm about to say in this book. That's totally fine, but I encourage you to go through those prompts and take some time with these concepts because it's hard to go forward without carefully thinking this part through. You've been warned . . .

Okay, so let's move on to a more focused question: What are the top 20 things you need? And when I say *need*, I mean need for a good life. Do you need to be a millionaire, or would a good life still be encompassed at $200,000? Do you need the McMansion, or is a safe neighborhood for your kids to play more important? Do you need your equal and capable partner to be six foot three or would a short king who treats you like a queen suffice?

I'm not saying to downgrade your dreams, but when I asked myself this, I wrote out a list and had to refine it quite a bit. Now, 20 might be a lot, so if you don't get to 20, that's okay because we are going to whittle that list down to 5 anyway. I had about 37 and had to squeeze it down. Once I had the list of 20, I read it over. I knew that family, health, and financial security were all important to me. But when I thought about organizing my life according to this list, the path still felt unclear. Having too many Maxims felt like a lot to carry around, and when I looked at the people close to death and what was important to them, the list was in fact very short. They wanted to be themselves, to live comfortably, and have good relationships with their loved ones. They weren't talking about their fancy car, house, or anything material at all. It came down to love and self.

My list was cluttered. Maybe I could achieve all these things, but it would be hard to keep track of, and I had a hunch my energy would be scattered trying to check all these things off. It felt like it would send me scrambling rather than center me in my decisions and actions. How about fewer things sorted into broader, more open-ended categories. Maybe my top five things? I tried again. Underlying all my thoughts was the question that became a drumbeat after my aunt's death: *What is a good life? What does it mean for me to live well?*

Here's what I came up with.

1. Health and wellness
2. Time with family and loved ones
3. Creative inspiration and travel
4. Passions achieved
5. Financial security

I had the list. Or a list. At least a draft of my Maxims, but I still needed to know what each one would look like. So, I took them one by one and thought through what each one would mean, adding little notes under each heading. Romantic partners and having a family used to be the top two until I got it, and now that has been shaped into time with those loved ones.

1. Health and Wellness

I want to feel good and have enough energy to give myself what I need. I want to be able to express my boundaries and surround myself with supportive people.

2. Time with Family and Loved Ones

This is time to interact with each other, build our relationships, and build core memories. It's engaging with someone who loves me, appreciates me, and supports me. It means feeling taken care of and being seen, a safety and stability along with deep love. A depth of connection.

3. Creative Inspiration and Travel

I want to experience the world in its beauty and let that inspire new ideas and ways of thinking.

4. Passions Achieved

I want my career endeavors to be recognized and successful in a way that my passions and achievements can help not just me but the world.

5. Financial Security

To me this means not having to worry about basic needs like having a safe place to live, having heat in the winter, not worrying about a utility being shut off or how to buy groceries this week, being able to feel a sense of peace, and not constantly worrying about money.

I should mention that the Maxims intersect. A romantic partner becomes part of my family. In fact, he did. Time with family overlaps with travel. We can build core memories on a summer trip to a cabin in the woods. And I have to be healthy enough to be able to enjoy this time. But even overlapping, the categories still give me a clear anchor as I make decisions day by day in terms of how I spend my time and where I put my energy. I had my five.

Are there other things I want and desire (sometimes with soul-crushing urgency)? Of course. A best-selling book, a house full of character that wasn't always a fucking mess, living in the South of France in a stone house on a hill overlooking the ocean . . . duh. Sign me up. I'd revel in every one of them. But I don't need them to live a good life, and a good life, remember, is what I'm after. I know I certainly don't need to manifest more. I don't need to compare myself to someone else's story or timeline. I don't need clout or status. I don't need someone else's approval: "Wow, now you've really made it." (I already had that, actually, a few times.) I don't need to impress anyone.

If my years were full of travel and creative inspiration, time with my family including a romantic partner, and I got myself to a healthy physical and secure financial situation, I would call that a good and meaningful life.

So, now let's turn to you. Before we get to the mystical and fantastical, we need to start with the practical. Perhaps you want to start with 20 Maxims, like I did, and then pare it down. Do you have your markers? Or the mind-map app? A simple pen and paper will do. Or open your laptop. Use the notes feature on your phone or your favorite journal. Whatever gives you a kind of dreamy, associative feel. You could turn on some music. I know I said we weren't getting to candles yet, but use whatever makes your space feel inviting.

What are the top 20 things you need to feel you are living a good life? It's totally okay to write some things down and cross them out. There's no time limit. Take a walk and come back to it. Make some tea and sip it slowly while you close your eyes and let the ideas come to you.

When you have your list of 20, or close to 20, look over it, and circle or highlight 5 that are the most essential. See if a few could be combined and have the same theme. Copy these to a separate list and call it your Maxim Top 5. And remember, don't worry. I'm not going to hold you to them. In fact, I'll be so happy to see you learn more about who you actually are that you go back and make changes to this list. What's cool is once you have them in writing, you can observe your behavior and figure out whether it matches your true Maxims. Is your day-to-day life aligned with your Maxims for a Good Life? This question lies at the heart of the Meaningful Manifestation process, which is learning about yourself and continuing to evolve. This is what I mean by Expansion. We'll come back to this question about alignment in later chapters.

For now, just know that to expand, we have to learn to pause. We don't get a lot of pauses in our lives. If one comes along, we almost always have our phone to start scrolling through whatever will entertain us out of sitting with the discomfort of slowing down. But it's in those pauses that we can find clarity, better access to what it is we think we want. By putting our desires out there, we ask the universe to help us define and redefine what we want.

And the universe will answer. It always does, which we will talk about later.

Is Your Desire Authentic?

Let's dive deeper into our desires so we can figure out what's behind them. It's important to figure out if we're seeking something because we truly want it and it aligns with our life purpose or if we're seeking something based on external messaging.

Look through each item on your Maxims for a Good Life list and ask yourself these questions: Is this coming from my heart, or is it a response to pressure from parents, friends, teachers, romantic partners, social media, or some other outside force? If it's from the heart, it's authentic. If it's from outside, it's inauthentic.

Sometimes it's easier to rule out inauthentic desires. Inauthentic desires are ones that have been pressed upon us. Think about influencers. They're everywhere. (I am kind of one myself.) We hope to motivate and inspire people, promoting a crystal that is going to help with grounding, a better way to communicate with your partner, or where to get the best dupe on a designer bag. Our followers are therefore receiving constant messaging from us. Some of the ideas and lessons may align with your life purpose; others might not.

We live in the capitalistic mecca, and consumerism is driven by telling us that we need things that we don't. Buy this, buy that, and then you will be happy. Get your face scalped to death to look like your favorite celebrity and then you will be beautiful—which they promise will make you happy, right? Ever heard of Instagram face? We are watching society increasingly push and press us into pretty little boxes marketing happiness as the end goal while profiting off our insecurities. And that pressure is nothing to scoff at. Once we start to see it everywhere, if we're not careful, we will be convinced that we too need the next thing that they are selling.

Is "everyone" clamoring for something, or does "everyone" have a certain purse and that's why you want it? Can you step back and determine whether a desire is coming from inside you? (I think I'm a bit of an outlier here. If everyone has something, I typically don't want it because of my rebellious nature. But that's still being defined by an external force. That means I still need to pause and try to get to the root of what would serve my best and highest good.)

Let's use a simple example. If you haven't eaten in three days, you need food. That's clearly an authentic desire. It needs to be met. But if you want a fourth cookie at the end of the night, that may come out of loneliness. That fourth double-fudge pecan nut crisp may be filling a void or patching up a wound and is not in your highest good.

Let's take it one step further. Look at the body "trends" that we have been seeing lately. First, we grew up where it was a sin to have your butt look big and now hear about women dying on the operating table because they got BBLs in another country on the cheap. They were *dying* to have a bigger butt, people. Why? Because the media we watch has convinced us that we would be happier, more attractive, and more desirable if we looked that way. And guess what? The pendulum swings again, and now all we hear about is Ozempic and how everyone is losing weight and that body acceptance has gone out the window and heroin chic is "in." First, let me say that your body is not a trend. Second, someone outside of ourselves is dictating what we should want or look like, and it is time we all stopped drinking the Kool-Aid. Affirming your authentic desires is an act of downright rebellion in this day and age. What do you want when you strip off the layer that outside influences have put on you?

So, the idea is to take desires one by one and vet them. Let's say one Maxim for a Good Life on your list is to be a parent. Okay. Let's hold the idea of being a parent and examine it.

Is being a parent in alignment with who you are and what you really want?

Did this desire come from inside you?

Did it come from your parents? From friends or society?

Did it come from messages you got about parenthood?

Is it from images you have seen of a mom influencer making sourdough bread at dawn as she gazes at her backyard chickens?

Do you enjoy your sleep and free time?

Are you asking out of a wound or a need?

Are you wanting this to shape someone into a version of yourself or to have someone to love you unconditionally?

Are you comfortable letting a being come into this world and be exactly who they are, even if it's at odds with what you expected?

That's just the start of some of the questions that would be necessary to take the time to vet out where the desire of becoming a parent is coming from. If you find a desire that feels like it is coming out of a wound, take the time to explore it further. We might feel we need a partner, job promotion, or child to validate us because we feel unlovable. We might want our children to behave because we fear we weren't good enough as children. When a wound is the origin of a desire, typically there can be a misinterpretation of whether or not something is an authentic need.

Wanting a certain amount of money to feel safe might come from a place of rational thought. Enough money will allow you to get needed repairs on your car, visit the doctor when necessary, and buy new shoes when your old ones are showing wear. But if you have plenty of money to support your life and still feel a burning desire to work 60 hours a week because you are terrified you don't have enough money for a neo-Baroque house on the coast of France and fear never having it, the desire could be coming from a wound.

I use this example from my own life because I have had this desire for a long time that one day I would live in France. I would learn the language fluently, eat all the good bread, drink the Sancerre with my meal like it was water, and live in a beautiful home doing the slow life near the coast of the Mediterranean Sea. It's incredibly romantic, ain't it? However, does that desire seep from any desire to escape the discomforts I see in my own country? Have I romanticized a place so much that my desire for it has amplified under false pretenses? Now, I believe it's an authentic desire that I have vetted many times over, but does this desire hold the linchpin to whether I live a good life? I don't think it does. Does that make it a need? No, it does not. It's an authentic want.

And those are okay too—they are more than okay! They are the little surprises that make life enjoyable. But being able to understand that it's not a need but a want means that I have that desire in a different category.

We often conflate the two.

Do you need to have children to have a good life? You might, according to your own Maxims of what a good life means to you. Some, after the difficult process of trying to conceive (which can still be painful to their heart having gone through that experience) might find out that they have a beautiful life and possibly even more beautiful than they would have had with children.

Another way to help make the distinction (when it's not as obvious as a fourth cookie) is by considering the feeling you have when you hold this desire in your heart. An authentic desire feels like a match. It is what we would call vibrationally in alignment. Working toward it feels like flow. On the other hand, inauthentic desires feel out of alignment. The opposite of flow. Trudging uphill. When we're trying to call something into our life that was not meant for us, these shadowy aspects of ourselves can be revealed. The wounding can show itself and ask us the hard questions like, *Is this what you really want?* This is part of the learning process, and we should see this as an opportunity to learn.

For example, when I was in my early 20s, a lot of my friends were getting married. It was basically a proposal-out-of-college-and-kids-by-25 kind of model. I hadn't had a serious boyfriend in a while and felt left out of life, like I was behind. That feeling of other set me on a path to pursue a relationship with someone I met on an interview who was 5,000 miles away. Y'all, I did the 90-day fiancé-ship before it was a twinkle in the show's producer's eyes. I chased and chased this relationship when it could have easily been over after my first visit. I wanted something so badly that I couldn't see the warning signs the universe had been sending me all along. On my first visit, there was a miscommunication about whether it was allowed to take photos in the museum, this place he was excited to show me. I couldn't read the language, but I saw a big photo that had a camera x'd out and bold letters that started with *nie*, which translated to "no." So, not wanting to get in trouble, I put my camera away, and my ex assumed that I thought I was too good for their museum, didn't ask questions, and gave me the silent treatment for the three-hour tour! With no explanation. This was horrible—I couldn't speak to anyone for clarity. He even bought himself lunch and sat away from me while I fumbled to ask for food from a menu I couldn't read and paid for with money I had no good idea the currency of. And this was before translation apps and international cell service. I felt like, what could I have possibly done for him to switch up on me so quickly? I couldn't fathom how I may have offended him, and it left me pursuing him despite his bad treatment. I wanted affirmation that we were going to be okay. He didn't speak to me even after I started crying except to say, "Big girls don't cry." What the actual fuck? I couldn't see it then because I was so desperate to fill in the gap. What's great is the universe gave me chances to see what wasn't in alignment for me and gave me many chances to opt out of this, but I stayed the course. And the universe finally gave me what I wanted. But it took me on a long path toward self-love and unfortunately maimed me with trauma that took a lot of time to work through. I breezed past the stop signs because my desire was being driven by a wound: that I was unlovable, that I was undesirable, and that no one would see the benefit of having me in their life. So, then I clung for dear life to the first person who saw me as valuable (well, he did get a green card out of it), but we had a five-year marriage that was very challenging and taught me some major lessons that I could have done without, if I'm being real with you.

It wasn't that I wanted to be married at that point in my life. It was just expected of me, and the pressure of religious purity and everyone telling you about the baby clock affected my 21-year-old mind. If I had lived in a place where young women were focused on their career instead of engagement rings, maybe things would have been different, but we can't go back in time. I just got the opportunity to look at that time and who I really was to know what I wanted at the time, but didn't feel I could express it due to the pressure around me. I didn't want to be left out or be the outlier (which is likely why I'm so rebellious now).

If you found any inauthentic desires on your list, remove them, and return to your Top 20 (a.k.a. your Maxims for a Good Life Rough Draft). Which one(s) pop out as most aligned? Read it over. Which ones give you a feeling that you want to feel? Bring it over to replace the desire you x'd out, and go through the vetting process once again. Do this as many times as necessary until you have a top five list that feels right and aligned.

(For now.)

So, you have your list and pared it down to your top five. You've now vetted each one. If you spotted any inauthentic desires, you've replaced them.

These are your priorities, your Maxims for a Good Life. Pretty cool, huh? Now you know how to move forward.

In the next chapter, you'll consider where you are starting. And then you'll move on to finding out what you want. Asking for what you want and moving through the process of receiving it gives you a chance to refine your ask. Each time you refine your ask, you get a chance to re-center yourself. And maybe that is, after all, what we're seeking?

To keep moving forward while continually re-centering. To find our North Star. Once we find it, we know which direction to turn. Meaningful Manifestation is about finding that center so we can be the best stewards of our time.

Open Yourself Up to Flexibility

Okay, so we may be able to determine that something is an authentic desire, innate to us. But we still don't always know what is meant for us in this lifetime. Maybe you think you want to be a mother, but you are meant to be a mother figure to students that you teach. Or perhaps you become the favorite aunt in the family, pouring all the energy you saved not having kids into your nieces and nephews. Sometimes the thing you're holding looks differently than you originally thought. We have to be open to that possibility.

Another possibility is that you have adopted a false timeline around *when* you're supposed to have accomplished something or arrived at a certain point. It may be that you will have your dream career and you will have a baby, but at a different time than you're imagining. It might mean that my house on the coast of France is an after 60 kind of thing and not a right now kind of thing (I'm punching air right now at the thought that I would have to wait that long, but, hey, we are all human).

There's a phrase I like to say on this subject often: "What's meant for me won't miss me."

What's meant for you won't miss you.

If it's supposed to happen, it will. If the universe has it in store for you, it's on its way. Maybe tomorrow, maybe in a quarter century, but it's coming. That means you can kind of relax about this stuff. Action may be required, but Meaningful Manifestation is not hunched over, hustling, rushing with a lot of angst and micromanaging.

Meaningful Manifestation is light, airy, spacious, and unhurried. A deep breath. A contented sigh. Openness and often neutrality. And all these things take time.

That is the feeling we want to embody. That is the spirit we want to bring forward. Surrender. Openness to receiving.

Universe, what do you have for me?

Doesn't that feel so light? So easy? Like I can loosen my death grip, and something outside of myself may be operating in a higher knowledge than I know of right now to align things in their proper timing to make the most of that experience. Imagine that I get that house on the coast right now. My children then have to uproot their lives, go to a new country, learn a new language, and perhaps have a bad experience in school because they are different (they might have that anyway, but stay with me). Maybe because I don't live in a silo, there are different ways in which our lives intersect that change the timing of these wishes and desires. Maybe age 60+ would be far better with adult children who can make their own choices and not resent having to be dragged into the romanticized version of my dream.

Maybe instead of buying a home, we are gifted one by a faithful listener of my show (hint hint) or maybe the book sales are so great that I don't have to settle on our vision, and we get to create a real-life dream. We don't know how time could bless the situation that we are asking for.

To achieve that state, we must be open to experiencing something in a different version or according to a different timeline than we may have predicted or expected. Manifestation is not a formula that works the same way every time.

And I don't think it would be enjoyable if it did. It would feel a bit rote, don't you think? Mechanical, when what we're going for is something a bit more . . . magical.

If you're feeling tired, worried, obsessive, and anxious, you might draw more of those feelings and experiences into your life purely based on perspective. Not that the universe would bring more bad into your life based on your thoughts because I believe the universe is completely neutral, but you'd sure see it that way. According to Anaïs Nin, "We don't see things as they are, we see things as we are." Each person filters the world through their own perceptions. Personal bias will always be a thing and in fact prevent us from ever truly being objective. This is how we manifest more good or more bad because our attention pursues it when it comes to how we feel about our lives.

If you're feeling hopeful, light, and aligned, you will create a vibrational match for yourself with those energies. A sense of security and stability will bring relationships and friendships into your life that are secure and stable because you will notice them and be more open to whatever frequency you participate with the most. You create the cycles. You can release yourself from the cycles you want to avoid. You invite the cycles in which you want to participate.

I like home projects. I love home decor and making a home feel rich and beautiful. Since I work from home, this is a high priority. But because I'm often scouring Instagram for home influencers, projects, and the like, I can often quickly experience discontent with my own home. Watching a 13-second reel transformation of someone's home makes me believe that it should happen fast, while I'm still looking at painter's tape applied three years ago on the ceiling of our unsuccessful kitchen renovation. I start to feel upset that I don't have a beautiful, bright kitchen that I love cooking in and even feel shame when others come to visit. But recently I was selling a chandelier we had on Facebook marketplace, and this woman came over to pick it up. She came into our foyer and just lost it. "Look at these crown moldings! Is that original travertine? These marble floors are beautiful! Are you an interior designer? Can I see the rest of the house?" Mind you, she's a complete stranger, so I didn't let her see too much but walked her around. When she entered our kitchen and I told her our plans for it, she said, "Wow, this house is just so special. They don't make them like this anymore. You are very lucky."

You are very lucky. Wow. I hadn't seen it that way because my focus was only on what I didn't have, not the beautiful home we *get* to live in. No matter how beautiful we end up making our kitchen, I might be apt to get on with the next project because I'm being flooded with inauthentic messaging constantly to continue the cycle. Just having someone new come in gave me eyes to see what I had was already complete, beautiful, and enough in its own right (painter's tape and all).

Vulnerability

If you want to change your life, you need to open yourself to how your life can change. It may be obvious, but it's not easy to welcome vulnerability. It takes practice. Typically, there will be resistance. To determine your Maxims for a Good Life, you have to really *look* at your life, yourself, and your wounds. It can be a painful process, this coming into awareness. And the vulnerability continues along the entire Meaningful Manifestation path because you have to be vulnerable to hope for something that you really want and not long for something an influencer says you should want or the kind of relationship your parents want for you. Those desires come with built-in protections because they're not about the real you. When you get to the real you, and what the real you wants, it can feel a little exposed.

The real me wanted a divorce from my ex the first year we were together. It challenged my ideas of what I thought would happen for my future. It was met with pressure from my parents to stay the course like they did. It came with judgment (for and against) that had me frozen exactly where I was because the process of stepping into what I really wanted meant that people would be hurt and disappointed and even change how they saw me. The day I asked for a divorce was the most vulnerable and exposed I ever felt; I almost wanted to take the words back. I didn't want anyone to be upset with me, and I was afraid to claim the real me and what my intuition had been screaming at me since the first day we met.

When we get caught up in our stories, we tell ourselves it can be difficult to break. I was caught up in a story where I just wanted someone to love me, but because I didn't love myself, I married someone that I now believe never truly loved me. To leave this marriage was to admit that I was wrong about him and admit to my friends that they were right since the beginning. That was a humbling experience to then shatter my life as I knew it in order to march toward what I authentically wanted. That wiped the slate bare, and I had to ask myself, "What do I want?" Sometimes we don't know! Mostly because of the messaging we are having to pry off ourselves with a crowbar. We have to also know that it's okay to want what we want when we may have had someone else tell us we can't have that thing. Now, this doesn't apply to murderers, criminals, and so on because they are inflicting their desires on someone else and violating that person's free will. That's an infringement. I know that's obvious, but I had to say it as it's the only caveat here. But I've been told numerous times that the goal I had was silly or unattainable, and so I searched for something others wanted for me. 'Scuse my language but that's bullshit. As an adult, it's your free will to discover what stands out to you and speaks to your soul. You also have the free will to pursue it.

Self-Sabotage

There is often some type of sacrifice involved in achieving what we want. Take health, for example. Exercise means a lot of huffing and puffing. Maybe that's some people's bag, but it's not everyone's. To keep your heart and cardio-vascular system in shape, you have no choice but to move through that dreaded huffing and puffing. Did you want to be sweaty, out of breath, and exhausted before you even start your day? Again, maybe some of you do, but I think I can speak for most of us when I answer with a resounding no. So, while you're there wincing on the elliptical, say this to yourself: the sacrifice I'm making is to get what I've been asking for this entire time.

That also means we have to believe we are worthy of what it is we're asking for. We've talked about messaging from other people. We also need to think about messaging from ourselves. Maybe there are areas in our lives where we are telling ourselves we don't deserve some of the things we want or even that it's not safe to want what we want.

When I was a blossoming teenager, I got a lot of unwanted attention from men that made me feel incredibly unsafe. I wanted attention but not *that* kind of attention, if you know what I mean. I was a solid stocky build in middle school, and none of the boys liked me. But when I lost weight, suddenly I was being noticed a lot more. At first it was great, but it slowly started to wane as I got older and the advances got more intense. I was 14 when I saw my first penis because a junior teammate of mine decided that I needed to know "what a real man looked like" by flashing me in the middle of track practice. I didn't ask for that; I didn't want that. And without going into too much detail beyond that, it got worse. I formed a core belief that it wasn't safe to be "attractive," and after I got into college and experienced even more dangerous things like that, I packed on the pounds.

No, it wasn't conscious but a coping mechanism my brain reasoned with that would keep me safe. I learned that I wasn't safe in the body I had, and I stopped what I was doing because my desire to be fit was working against a higher Maxim of safety.

So I sabotaged it. And often sabotage comes from this place. We have another Maxim fighting against what could possibly be our true desire. I can't make more money than my parents because it will make my family feel insecure. I need to be in a relationship because others will think something is wrong with me if I am not. I can't wear this dress on a date because he might think I'm sending him a signal that I'm not. We find ways out of being authentic to ourselves in the moment because a more important Maxim may be in play.

If we don't believe we are worthy, we'll be quick to listen to the wrong voice or even a bad experience, the one telling us to sit down and stop advocating for our health, career, or future.

A Few Last Words about Maxims

As you move through the process, you'll find that the Maxims help you make choices, create manifestations that align with your core values, cultivate greater clarity and purpose, and grow as a human. As we grow, we get to know ourselves better, and that clarity means we can't help but grow even more.

What do you value, really? Often our values can be broken down into the feelings we want to feel. If you appreciate financial abundance, your value might be security or safety. If you want a romantic partner, your value might be intimacy or the feeling of love. If you participate in activism or charity, you might value empathy or justice. Learning the value underneath the desire will make it increasingly evident what you truly would like to manifest.

In the next chapter, we'll talk about your starting point (Inception), and we'll move on to setting your intentions for what you want to call into your life right now. These manifestations will grow out of the Maxims for a Good Life you've established here, and they will help you arrive at a place where you're not constantly chasing. Where you can be.

You may even get to a place where you realize you don't need the things you thought were essential. If that happens, don't worry; it just means you're expanding. You can always come back to this chapter and refine your Maxims. They are guideposts. You may find that you're not following your guideposts. Let's say, for example, that you have time with family as a Maxim, but every chance you get, you meet up with friends or join a new activity rather than have an evening at home. Then this simply means you have an opportunity. Your behavior is not aligning with your Maxim, so which do you want to change?

46

The choice is up to you.

That's the wonderful truth at the heart of this work—it's up to you. It's spiritual and it's fantastical and it's sometimes hard to grasp all of it. But at the center is what you want out of this life. Your wishes, your dreams, your actions, and your choices and bringing them into better alignment as you bring more meaning and purpose into your life. We only have so much attention and energy. Let's focus it on what truly matters and let go of forces that have been holding us back. This is how we move away from aimlessness toward authenticity. This is how we find the path toward Meaningful Manifestation. This is how we gain the perspective to move forward after disappointment or even devastation. This is how we become more present in the lives we have.

Chapter 4

Inception

Where Are You Starting?

Start here.

If you're going on a road trip, it's important to know where you're starting from. Otherwise, you won't know which way to turn when you come to the first intersection. Let's say you and I both want to get to LA, but I'm starting in Kansas City and you're starting in Brooklyn. If we travel at the same speed, I'll get there first. Does that make me better than you? Of course not. It's just laws of time and space. My starting point was farther along than yours.

The analogy might seem ridiculously simple, yet when it comes to manifestation, we often overlook this point. We compare ourselves to others, but we don't stop and consider that we did not start at the same place. We don't all have the same kinds of privilege and access.

Privilege comes in many different forms. It can happen along the dimensions of race, economics, intelligence, physical ability, trauma we've experienced, vulnerability to depression, and whether we live under a stable government, among others. The differences show up most clearly in race, gender, sexual orientation, and economic class—on a systemic level, we face different roadblocks depending on our diversities within the system. We're working collectively as a society to address these injustices, but in the context of you starting your IMAGINE journey, it's important just to acknowledge that the differences exist. Perhaps activism in this area will be one of your Maxims. (We'll get to that later.) For now, let's acknowledge that some people have more access to what they want to manifest due to privilege based on the color of their skin, how much money they make, or what body they were born in.

Some people are born into wealth and some into families struggling to pay the rent on their apartment. Again, this may seem obvious, but if we're trying to access a frequency that will attract wealth, we can't pretend we all have the same access to it. I think this point is where a lot of people lose hope on their manifestation journey. I hear from people in my circles all the time who say they tried it and "it didn't work." Well, what didn't work? And what exactly did you try? And did you acknowledge your starting point? It's a principle that needs to be applied, not a magic pill.

I know a lot of people feel like they did all the things they were told to do, and they're still not happy. In fact, as I wrote about in the Introduction, this was *me*. But that was before I grasped what manifestation could truly mean and how healing it can be when we approach it in a different way. I'm not saying my way is the only way, but after seeing damn near all the ways, this is the only way that for me made the most sense to ground us in reality while using a principle of the universe that could grant us the changes we seek.

So, taking time to think about our Inception Point grounds us into our everyday life. It also gives us compassion for other people and for ourselves as well. It reminds us to be flexible. If we don't have as much access as someone else to economic opportunities, there may be many more layers we need to go through before we find that financial security we're seeking.

None of it is fair. These are just our circumstances, the nature of where we are on this human plane. The hand we've been dealt. It seems silly to get upset if I pull up to Laguna Beach before you do (but I'll for sure save you a spot).

If you don't seem to be drawing in the things you want right now, it could be that the stars are in retrograde. There might be different waves of energy circling the universe than the ones you need. It could be that it's not the best timing for your life, and you wouldn't want to eat an apple pie before it's done cooking, right? You wouldn't want to manifest from a place of hunger that would cause you to settle for uncooked dough versus a golden-brown crust. Who's hungry?

So, much of our work depends on asking questions and giving ourselves the space and time to answer.

Ask yourself, Where am I starting?

If you have less privilege in whatever area you're trying to expand into, I want to invite you *not* to beat yourself up. I want to remind you also that manifestation is seasonal. One of the cool things, I think, is that this whole process draws patience into our lives. If we accept that this whole process is about healing, we have to accept that it will take time because healing takes time. Seeking takes time. Expansion takes time. Transformation takes time. Coming into alignment takes time. Meaning takes time.

I was once sitting in meditation and was brought this really intense thought about time. In the mediumship work I've done, I've also researched a ton about NDEs (near-death experiences). Many of the ancestors I have spoken with from the other side have mentioned that there is no time on the other side. That everything happens all at once and whenever you focus your attention on something, that BAM! It's right there in front of you in your consciousness.

During this meditation, my guides spoke to me about just how fun it is to be in the physical earth plane because we get to see things play out in a linear fashion—something we don't experience on the other side. So, yes, waiting is in fact *fun* for our souls because it's something new and exciting we don't experience on the other side. Would you believe that? We came in a density-like structure to know more fully how beautiful the creation process is when we get to see it in all its stages. That the wait and the process of manifestation is a slower process that our soul actually loves because as only a few people know on this earth, life is boring when you get everything you want and takes you on this endless manifestation journey of accruing more and more that never makes anyone feel sated.

It's like watching a movie—who wants to know the end before we watch it? It's why we have spoiler alerts on every commentary of every show or movie to warn the listener or reader that the ending is about to be revealed. And people *hate* that. Similarly, we are here in this matrix putting together these incredible timelines, and our souls don't want to ruin the ending for us (or them). Hard to conceive, but it makes sense to me why on this side we expect everything to happen at once and find it frustrating as hell when we have to wait on nearly anything. You know how you feel when you are watching a movie with someone, and they spill a spoiler? Straight to jail. A criminal offense because you want to ride the wave of how it's going to play out. You like the suspense . . . except when it comes to your own story. But your soul is excitedly watching it all unfold, and it loves the seasonality of manifestation.

What do I mean by seasonality when I talk about manifestation? Well, let's think of it in terms of the actual seasons. Let's say it's January, and you are ready for beach weather. You want to be sprawled on the sand with a cooler full of lemonade and salty snacks, ready to crack open your beach read. Well, if you live in Missouri, it doesn't matter how ready you are for summer. You're gearing up for your next bout of seasonal affective disorder because the sun is not going to come out tomorrow.

Maybe we are trying to draw in a romantic partner, and nothing seems to be working. Bad dates. Or a string of good dates and then getting ghosted out of nowhere. (I once went to France to spend time with a guy I was dating, and he ghosted me *during the trip*.) We're so let down and frustrated that we start thinking the right match doesn't exist. What happens next is we cut ourselves off from being vulnerable enough to continue to desire a romantic partner or don't think it's possible because it's too painful to wait. But maybe that partner is coming in summer. Maybe it needs to be flip-flop weather before you're going to even catch the first glimpse of this person. If you have the patience to wait and to stay open, you'll be open to receiving. Imagine that I started to tell people I didn't believe in summer anymore because it was taking too long, and now I'm throwing away all my summer clothes because it's easier for me to close my heart off than to wait the three to five months it's going to take to have what I want. You would tell me I was being belligerent. Why do we do that when it's something we want to manifest? "This doesn't work for me."

And that lack of openness will mean you are right because even though our manifestation isn't for sure coming during a particular time of year, it would come during a particular time of our life, if it's meaningful to you. I believe that we don't obtain meaningful desires if they aren't meant for us. Maybe that doesn't feel true to you, and that would be totally okay, but there is something in each manifestation that gives us expansion for our soul's desire to learn about ourselves. Sometimes a missed manifestation is more important to what our soul wants to learn rather than the obtaining of it. That's a painful thought but a true one, at least in my life. For instance, by moving forward with my ex out of desperation, I lost time with what I really wanted in a partner if I had been willing to wait. But it didn't escape me . . . it instead took me on a 10-year journey toward finding my worth and in hindsight that was so incredibly valuable despite the pain I endured.

Pushing and forcing is not the energy of allowing, and allowing is the energy of manifestation. If you notice a lot of stress and resistance, you're probably not in the best energy that will help you toward your goal. So, let's begin a gentle path with deep breaths and patience, knowing we have the power inside to get where we want to go. We're at the beginning. Just *beginning* to Imagine. What a great place to be.

There's a practical aspect to acknowledging where you are as well. You can study the steps someone else took and then you can think rationally about how they got where they are, taking into account their starting place and how it relates to yours. But keep an open mind because their way might not be your way. You might have a few detours or take a completely different route. The key is to be open because you never know what this road has in store, and remaining open will be very important.

Here are some questions to ask yourself. As in previous chapters, you can get out a journal, open a document on your laptop, or dictate into your phone. Whatever feels right.

Let's begin.

Where did you start?
What got you to this point currently?
How do you feel where you are?
What makes you want to change where you are?
What needs to change for this to happen?
How long do you think it will take to change?
(What are your expectations?)
What's kept you from changing it up to this point?
Are you ready to move forward?

The last question is a big one. If you're not ready, the universe won't be either. And lots of times, let's face it, the ego shows up. *Uh-oh, what's all this commotion?* the ego might say. *This is interfering with our homeostasis.*

Also, it's good to remember that things that are out of your control can be to your advantage or disadvantage. At the start, we don't always know. Take the time to honor your feelings and give them space to release. Acknowledge your feelings. By doing that, you can then move on to the next step. But acknowledging where you've felt hurt, unseen, or treated unfairly is where you need to start.

What If You're Feeling Despair?

I want to take a moment here to discuss what steps you can take if you feel stuck in frustration and even anger about the obstacles you face and, perhaps, the privilege you lack compared to others. Let's talk this through and get to the meat of it. If you know me from my podcast, you know I don't shy away from going deep, which will be necessary to find where you are.

Let me ask you this: What are you feeling? What has gotten in the way of your dreams so far? Are the forces systemic? It's natural to feel deep anger at unfair systems, and totally justified. All these feelings deserve space and acknowledgment.

Now, I want to ask you, are you willing to take your power back? Instead of allowing the energy to cycle and hold *you* back, can you become emboldened and empowered in a true state of knowing instead?

What do I mean by that?

Prove everybody wrong! *Stick it to them.* Come with *that* kind of defiant energy. Move the energy from feeling angry and stuck to deciding how *you* want to show up in this life. We want to move energy away from being angry at how we started or guilty about what we didn't do and direct that energy toward changing our lives now. How can you make the best of what you have right now? Let's embrace the energy of being emboldened and empowered!

I have a rebellious personality, right? If I'm at a stoplight and someone honks at me right when the light turns green, before I even have a chance to go, better believe I'm going to sit there for 10 seconds or even 30 seconds more for good measure because *you're not going to rush me.* When I was nominated for homecoming queen and one of the girls told me I had no chance of winning, I made sure to walk by and make eyes at her with my queen crown at the dance. Many of my Christian friends told me I was going to hell by using my oracle cards, and what did I do? Made it my career and bought this house with card-pulling money, honey (hear my snap, okay?). Regardless of whether this trait of mine is healthy (to be determined), I wasn't going to let life or anyone else tell me what I would be or wouldn't be doing in this life. No, babes, this was not the energy I was going to live my life.

But I will admit there were most definitely other areas where I had a real tough time doing this. Relationships was one of them. I had a large gaping wound and a pick-me-girl

56

attitude. I wasn't aware of where I was starting from and what wounds I needed to heal before I approached this equal and capable partnership. I had a lot I needed to shift in the way I saw myself and give grace to the space I started from such as the trauma I had endured, the unhealthy relationships I had, and most importantly the lack of self-love I had for myself.

We're shifting perspective. We're seeking clarity. We're not looking backward; we're looking ahead to where we want to go and how we want to prove those negative intrusive thoughts in our mind wrong.

This is your journey. It's not my journey. It's not the journey of your parents, your friends, your neighbor from two blocks over, or your high school youth pastor. It's *yours*. Unique to you. Just because you're not starting at the same place as someone else doesn't mean your dreams aren't possible and don't hold intense potential to be great outcomes in your life.

We're swimming away from murky waters that keep our real desires hidden. We're acknowledging and releasing guilt or anger at any system we feel is responsible— whether it's our parents, society, the patriarchy, or any other force or influence.

When we do this, accepting where we're beginning becomes an anchor. It centers and grounds us. Take a deep breath. (Another deep breath.) You can now begin. The true place of Inception is acceptance. It's about finding peace where you are. You might as well find it there, as you're not going to find it anywhere else.

Let's move forward with softness. Here's a quote from a blog post by Lisa Olivera called "Stay Soft" that feels like a gentle invitation to staying flexible and vulnerable in our journey: "Softening allows for possibility. Softness invites clarity back into the picture . . . Softness creates room.

Softness holds space. Softness releases what is stuck. Softness lets me be affected by life without being continuously punctured, gut-punched, pummeled by it."

Despite the fear and trauma I've experienced in relationships, I have made it a point to keep myself soft-hearted. I kept trying. If I had hardened myself and shut down, that would have meant closing myself off to future romantic possibilities. Instead, I stayed vulnerable. It wasn't easy. I was angry for a long time. But acknowledging the anger, giving space for the anger to be expressed, and allowing those emotions to be seen gave way to the grief and sadness I had experienced that gave me a chance to stay open. Sometimes when we don't acknowledge our feelings, we allow them to rot, and that scar closes the wound with the rot in it. We can't stay open while there's rot . . . so better out than in to give yourself a fighting chance to stay authentically vulnerable. Staying open allowed me to enter the most amazing, life-giving relationship. Pushing didn't get me there. Forcing didn't get me there. It was soft. Openness. Allowing. A mix of vulnerability and strength to move into a different space.

And speaking of moving into a different space, let's talk about the energy you surround yourself with, starting with what you consume. Not just food and drinks, but what do you read, what do you scroll on social media, what do you say to yourself out loud? What do you fill yourself with day in and day out? This is what I call Clean Up.

What we consume in our daily lives greatly affects how we think about ourselves and the world around us. Ever got in an algorithmic rabbit hole where you liked one video on canning and suddenly you keep getting more and more videos about prepping, bunkers, or the cataclysmic end of the world? Whew, suddenly you start feeling fearful about the world around you and might start stockpiling perishables and buying several generators in case the world goes out of power. Not a bad idea but suddenly it feels very true because you are now consumed. You are what you eat, and you are what you watch, read, and listen to as well.

Say it's something completely different. Say you get in a rabbit hole of fitness influencers and suddenly you think your body isn't good enough. Say you start seeing that everyone has a Stanley cup (not the hockey one), and suddenly now you think you need a $45 water bottle in every color. Sounds absurd but this is what is happening right now as I'm writing this. Maybe it's a constant stream of Islamophobia that makes you start to fear Muslim people. Or your favorite fashion influencer shows her closet and her latest bag that you feel you just have to have to be complete. Many of our fears, wants, and desires can come innocently from what we are consuming, and we are often being influenced in ways that we wouldn't even consent to if we were conscious of it.

Try putting more attention toward what you want to experience. Clean up your inner world so you can have a strong Inception Point. Are your habits bringing you closer to the space you want to be in? Or further away? What kind of environment do you want to be in? Are you cultivating routines that will allow you to create the environment you want? Are you cultivating energetic resistance or energetic embrace?

Journaling, therapy, and building healthy relationships are all practices we can call on to support ourselves here. Where does your thought life live? What do you spend the most time enjoying? All the content you consume can affect how you feel about yourself and the world, so be intentional here.

All these questions will help you start thinking about where you are now. They will help you come into a true state of knowing because we can't truly start from any-where else, so we may as well get clear on where we are.

As I was writing this, I was prepping for a mystic fair. I want my space to look different. I had this idea of what I wanted, but I had to be realistic about where I was starting from. I decided I wanted to go with a retro circus vibe, and I didn't have thousands to spend on a custom tent with silk canopy. But fortunately when I was working as a photographer, I became really good at the *dupe*. I would find something expensive and figure out a way to make it cheaply but still opulent and beautiful. For the fair, I got a tent for under $100 and put a ruffled pink bed canopy on top. Then I used a glue gun to attach tassels on the side. I made an embroidered banner that looked lush and ornate, and it was all from things I found for cheap and made. I had an idea for what I wanted, and I brought it into fruition.

Getting this tent ready reminds me of when I was in high school, and my friend, my sister, and I were dancing in this pep rally. My friend was super fashionable and always had on the best clothes, so she picked out what she thought we should wear for the rally. My sister and I couldn't afford this outfit. It was a flag top and there was a painted motif on the jeans. My mom was like, "I can make that." She got us some tank tops and jeans from Walmart and went to town. Thanks to my mom's creativity, I never saw us as poor. To this day, if we see something we want that might be out of our reach financially, we find a way to make it.

Anyway, we came to school in homemade outfits that looked better than what my friend was wearing and rocked that pep rally with confidence. It was a great lesson: we could use our creativity to figure out how to make things. This was training for manifestation. We may not have money to buy the tent or pep rally outfit of our dreams, but we have something even better: creativity and intuition. The ability to bring something new into the world exactly from where we started. Isn't that what manifestation is?

People asked me where I got all my stuff for the tent, and when I told them I made it, it was more satisfying because I may not have had much experience making those things but because I believed I could, nothing was out of my reach. You may be coming from humble means, but you are a badass creative and see different ways to make the same thing. You may be coming from a broken relationship that killed your self-esteem but are determined to rise out of that wound and learn how to be authentically yourself. You may be denied for that investor loan because you are a victim of systemic racial profiling, but you have strong determination to keep asking until you get a yes and prove the haters wrong. Nothing, my dear, is out of your reach when you know where you are starting from.

Chapter 5

Manifestation

What Do You Want?

*Pretend that this is the time of
miracles and we believe in them.*

— EDWIDGE DANTICAT

Here we are at the heart of the book. You picked up this book because there is something you want, right? You want it so much, it's running through your mind constantly. Maybe it's keeping you up at night. Filling pages of your journal. Maybe it comes up in every conversation with your best friend. Or maybe it's something you never told anyone.

Traditional methods of manifestation haven't worked. It's possible you've achieved dreams and acquired things you longed for, but, like me, you look around at your life and still don't feel happy. You know there has to be more. There has to be a way to find meaning in your days. Somewhere, still out of reach, there's a good life that is yours to lead but that you are still not leading. So, you picked up this book.

And you were right. That good life that's yours to lead is out there, and it's within reach. If you've made your way through the last few chapters, you've figured out your Inception Point and determined Your Maxims for a Good Life. You know where you are and what you want. Maybe

63

you've already made changes to what you want as you've reflected on that. Hopefully you've gained greater clarity about your starting point. Maybe you've already revised your Maxims for a Good Life.

So you are ready to ask. And I have a piece of advice for you at this stage in the journey: be mindful of what you ask for, because once you commit to your big dreams, you will be called to level up. Leveling up is exciting, but it does require courage. Sometimes we block our own tasks because we're not ready to level up. This happens a lot, and that's perfectly normal. That's why this process of Meaningful Manifestation is about the work of getting to know who you are and what you want. If nothing else, that's what I hope you come away with. Not everything about yourself. You can't learn that all from one book! But I hope you begin that beautiful process of learning about yourself and learning to trust yourself. It lasts a lifetime.

While I want you to pursue your desires with intention, I also want you to allow the universe some agency in terms of *how* those manifestations come into your life. Another thing that gets in the way a lot of the time is our need to control HOW something happens. We're afraid that our manifestations may not come without us taking every detail and micromanaging it into oblivion. This goes back to the idea of softness from the previous chapters. Gentleness. Allowing. Opening up. Receiving.

Last summer I wanted to book a vacation to LA. I booked the tickets, but we didn't have the funds at the time to do the rest of the trip. It was frustrating, I'm not gonna lie. But as I dreamed about palm trees and long sunsets over the ocean, I was able to take a pause and ask myself, *What is it you're actually seeking, Alea?*

I knew it wasn't the specific need to put my feet in the ocean or hike in the canyons. So, I let myself sit with that question: What do you need at this moment?

And the answer came.

I was trying to manifest time away that felt restorative. I decided I wasn't going to hold tight to the need to control how that happened. Maybe LA would have been full of traffic and crazy expensive. Maybe it wouldn't have been restorative, let alone in my best and highest interest.

What I needed to do was get clear on what I wanted to bring in—a restorative escape—and surrender to the universe. I knew this answer. I know this answer. And yet, like many of you, I imagine, I need to learn and remind myself of it again and again.

The expectations that the vacation *had* to be in LA was causing me suffering. It was stressing me out, as I was checking prices and trying to make plans without the cash to make it work. If I loosened my grip on what I was asking for, I could minimize a lot of my suffering. In fact, by doing this, I could reduce a lot of my stress *right now*, the very stress I'm trying to get away from.

Having a death grip on an expectation can cause us a lot of pain, especially if the ask we are making is tied into an idea of what would make us happy in the moment versus what would actually make us happy.

I canceled our plane tickets and instead booked a week in a beautiful cabin by the lake in Arkansas, where it's so quiet after the sun goes down, you can just melt into the deafening silence. It was literally in the middle of nowhere with no distractions, and the nearest grocery store was 45 minutes away. Who knew that something simpler and less glamorous would be exactly what I needed? I was afraid that we wouldn't have as good of a time, but the quiet time in nature away from the city was more beautiful than expected.

One of my all-time favorite quotes comes from *101 Essays That Will Change the Way You Think* by Brianna Wiest. She says:

> You believe that creating your best life is a matter of deciding what you want and then going after it, but in reality, you are psychologically incapable of being able to predict what will make you happy. Your brain can only perceive what it's known, so when you choose what you want for the future, you're actually just recreating a solution or an ideal of the past. When things don't work out the way you want them to, you think you've failed only because you didn't recreate something you perceived as desirable. In reality, you likely created something better, but foreign, and your brain misinterpreted it as "bad" because of that. (Moral of the story: Living in the moment isn't a lofty ideal reserved for the Zen and enlightened; it's the only way to live a life that isn't infiltrated with illusions. It's the only thing your brain can actually comprehend.)

This quote drastically changed my life because I was (and still am, if I'm being honest) the expectations queen. In many instances, I have done this very thing where the outcome I didn't plan turned out to be exactly what I needed and often better that what I could have planned for.

Impatience can trip us up.

Expectations trip us up.

Fear can trip us up.

But sometimes we're not thinking too big; we're thinking too small.

Our fear of failure also gets in the way of our clarity because sometimes we will settle for what seems easiest to achieve versus the big thing we really want. The confusion is not about what our heart wants but the pain we are worried we might feel if we don't get our true heart's desire.

Either way, action is required. You've heard people say if you're looking for a partner, you need to "put yourself out there." You do. You can't hole up in your house, streaming movies, and expect to meet someone that way. That's not what I mean by softness, by ease. But maybe you don't need to be on a dating app. Maybe you can join a club. Attend a reading. Go to after-work drinks and see who shows up.

Let's even take this book. For my first book, I sent queries to 38 publishers and heard nothing back. I printed it myself and sent it to friends, and it was a huge flop. A $14,000 flop. Talk about a letdown. All the time and effort and resources I poured into that flop! Painful. With my second book, I tried not to let my expectations get too high. I wrote it myself and got an editor. I self-published again, but it didn't do very well. All right, cool, fine. If it helps five people, then it was worth it, right? I still knew I wanted to write a damn book that people would actually read. I knew I had a few books in me.

I still wanted to write a badass book, but I loosened my expectations about what that process was going to look like and how that was going to go. Fast-forward five years, and here came Amy the editor from Hay House in my DMs. I don't usually read all my DMs and often have scammers in the mix. She asked me if I wanted to collaborate on a book. Did I want to write a book? Hell, yes! What was crazier is that I didn't have to do much this time around to make that happen because I was much more experienced in allowing energy to enter my life. Manifestation is about receiving.

I took action. I wrote two books. Then I handed things over to the universe. I didn't let the other "flops" hold much weight, but I could have and closed myself off to the possibility of trying this again. We do that sometimes when our disappointments hurt our feelings so badly that we sometimes never recover. Maybe it's rejection from someone we like, a rejection letter from a school we wanted to go to, a "we regret to inform you" letter from a job you were hoping to get. These things are painful when we put our hopes and dreams into something that doesn't pan out, but here I am writing this for one of the biggest spiritual publishing houses in the world, despite the harrowing disappointments of my past that prepared me for this opportunity. We have to practice seeing the larger picture for our lives.

Will this book sell enough for me to get another deal? Will I become this insanely well-published author, traveling across the country for speaking engagements and interviewed by daytime TV? And will I finally get to buy my European dream house?

I don't know. That's a lot of expectations. I can only take the actions I can take, loosen my grip on those expectations and about how things should go, and hopefully get more and more clarity around what it is I truly want and keep refining my ask as I go. Maybe this book will help only five people and maybe it will be a *New York Times* bestseller. Who knows? But if I put all my hopes and expectations into this thing, then I'm setting up for even more disappointment if I don't allow for this outcome to be flexible enough for the universe to give me what is in my best and highest potential.

I'm not here to teach you how to quick fix your life. I think soon enough we all realize nothing's going to quick fix our life. You might start a YouTube channel and become a millionaire in a day, and while that's great, it's likely not going to be a long-lasting trajectory. How would you handle all that fame overnight? How would you keep up with the content calendar without a proper team? Your career could end as fast as it started, realistically speaking. We're looking for fast fixes, which means avoiding pain. But pain is part of the experience. The two books I wrote that were flops? That was painful. And it led me here, to where I get to write the book you're holding in your hands. I know a lot more that I can put into this book in large part because of the pain I went through with the two other books. If I hadn't gone through a terrible marriage, I wouldn't be in a healthy, safe, loving one now. I wouldn't know how to communicate clearly. I wouldn't have learned how to talk myself out of the stories I tell myself when I'm hurt, that I don't matter, that I'm disposable, that people don't love me. (All the things that my wounding would have me believe.) I'm able to stop and say, wait, that's not what's happening here. I'm able to realize I have increasing control over how I see the situations in my life.

My two-year-old wants a Popsicle every time she goes to the fridge. Toddlers are snack queens—anyone with a toddler knows this. But she needs to know there is a limit and be allowed to have her feelings around this. Her stepsister wants to run to her and stop her from feeling upset, but what I am trying to teach both of them is that it's okay to have the big feelings and have the space to be upset. Within safe limits, it's perfectly okay to melt down, whether it's because you don't get the vacation you want or the reaction to your book you wanted, or something far more upsetting. (Like not getting the last strawberry pop.)

My baby girl is a toddler, so she has us to comfort her. We're there to reassure but not take away the chance for pain. If we take that chance away, she won't get the opportunity to learn how to regulate her emotions. I don't know if I'm Parent of the Year for doing this. But I want her to know it's okay to have uncomfortable emotions. There are going to be a lot of them during our time on this earth. She's learning how to deal with the horrifying phrase "all gone." To face the empty Popsicle box.

Let's not safeguard ourselves from the growth process that our soul came here to have in the first place.

Let's recognize that our timeline might not be the universe's timeline. The universe might be telling us something is "all gone" for now, and we have to deal with that. Manifestation was never about getting endless Popsicles from the universe.

Surrendering is letting go of something not in defeat but in expectation of it coming back in a different form, when we are ready. Surrendering is not giving up. It's not saying, "Okay I've hit my max capacity for waiting. I'm just going to give up so I don't have to feel the suffering of waiting." When people do this, they become hardened to the very thing they desire. They close themselves off.

Stay open. Surrender space. Recognize something may not happen on your timeline but that you might be surprised when you get a DM from someone handing you the very thing you've wanted for 15 years that you surrendered to but never gave up on.

This is a lifelong practice. It doesn't stop when you understand the principle of attraction. It doesn't stop when you learn my IMAGINE method. We're going to do this thing over and over. We're going to refine and redefine what we're asking for.

What do you want? Truly. The surprising part about this is that when I ask clients about what they want, they can often be puzzled like no one has ever asked them that question before. What happens if you don't know what you want?

My husband (then fiancé) and I were planning this gorgeous wedding. I was so excited to have enough money to have the wedding of my dreams with all the important people in my life. I had vision boards and mock-ups of what the space would look like to give the florist and planner, and it was going to be a vision! After getting most of the services booked, sending invitations, and having the dress on the way, I started to feel nervous that this event wasn't going to happen. We were having some extended family issues at the time, and it became such a problem that we ended up having to cancel the wedding. I was devastated. The texts flooded in, with people wondering if we were still together. The shame of all the plans that had fallen by the wayside (and the money) made everything worse. It wasn't even our fault, but it was clear we couldn't get married with the turmoil between our families to have the day we wanted.

A few months later, once the dust had settled, I started planning the new iteration of our wedding, but I was hesitant because I didn't know if something else like this would happen and couldn't take another heartbreak like that. I started thinking about what if we eloped and what that could look like. But because I had photographed some 750 weddings in my past, I kept thinking it had to be this big event, this elegant, epic affair. We ended up booking this amazing venue in Tulsa at the Philbrook Museum of Art. I was so excited because I knew the photos would be sooo gorgeous! But the planning started to become this animal I couldn't control, and I started circling the drain again about the stress it was causing me.

What did I want? I asked my husband "Do you want to just elope?" He said, "Yes, but what do you want? I want you to be happy with whatever we do." But I just didn't know. We went ahead with the big wedding plans since we already made the deposit, and once we started calculating how much just the freaking rental chairs would cost, I started to feel sick. I ordered new invitations for our completely new event, only to cancel it this time because I just didn't want to do it anymore. I just wanted to marry my best friend and have beautiful photos—that's it. I didn't care about or need all that other stuff. That single line of clarity led me to plan an intimate wedding in a nearby park with less than 30 people and barely any chairs or decorations. I planned it in nine days. YES, nine days!

It was the most beautiful affair. The pictures were gorgeous because they were filled with love. We flew to Paris for a honeymoon that involved even more beautiful photos. It was through the disappointment that I was able to refine my ask, leading me to what really mattered and what was going to be most meaningful to my life. What's even funnier is that I had shot so many weddings—big weddings—to know that's not what I wanted but succumbed to the pressure of everyone and their momma wanting to be included. We ultimately had to choose what was best for us. (My husband very much appreciated the much simpler event but didn't want me to be disappointed after seeing my big plans. Happy wife, happy life, I guess.)

Sometimes we have to go through all that disappointment to know what matters, what's meaningful to us.

What will you ask for?

Chapter 6

Anti-Belief

*When your dreams are bigger than the places you find
yourself in, sometimes you need to seek out your own
reminders that there is more. And there is always more
waiting for you on the other side of fear.*

— ELAINE WELTEROTH

Did I have to travel more than 9,000 miles to a small island
in Indonesia to discover my Anti-Belief?

I'm not sure.

But that's how it happened.

I was lying in savasana, the final, restorative pose for
a yoga session I'd completed with a small group of new
friends. As I lay on my mat, an image began to take shape in
my mind. It was 12-year-old me. I had been told by my par-
ents that I could not continue to take my gymnastics class,
and I was crushed. I was going to be the next Dominique
Dawes. Money was always tight in our household, and I
wanted to do a lot of things. We were too poor for me to be
the next Kristi Yamaguchi (ice skater), but when the YMCA
started offering $25 for each season of gymnastic class, my
mom saw an opportunity. She came home to tell me I was
going to start gymnastics, and I was so excited that I broke
out in hives, no joke. Crying and itchy from sheer excite-
ment, I was so stoked to finally get into my dream. But after
a few seasons, my parents couldn't afford to pay the $25

anymore, even though it was incredibly cheap. My coach still allowed me to come to class. The coach knew that we didn't have the money, but the coach had a promising student who had just figured out how to do a back handspring.

One day I came home with my report card, and I had gotten a C in my math class. My parents didn't know that I was dyslexic at the time, but they should have, given that my dad was as well. My dad looked at my report card and said, "Welp, your grades are slipping. I guess you're going to have to quit gymnastics."

What.

I started to boil with anger. One, because my grades were never made known as a contingency for doing gymnastics. Two, because every other grade was an A. Three, because I knew it wasn't about my grades; it was about the money. They were already nine months and $75 behind.

That was the moment I decided I needed to fend for myself. Perhaps it was a drastic reaction. But that's how my 12-year-old mind felt at the time. If I wanted things like new clothes or an after-school activity, I would have to get a job to pay for them. I couldn't rely on my parents or my teachers. And certainly not the universe.

It was all up to me.

That decision in sixth grade ushered in a long period of hypervigilance. I started my first job at Dairy Queen when I was 14, and I bought my first car when I was 15. I upgraded to a better-paying job at 16. I graduated high school with honors. Got into a private college by scholarships and mostly my own loans. I worked all through college to support myself to move out and live on my own by 19, graduating college with high marks despite a learning disability. Got my first salary job and bought my first house by 21, started my own photography business by 22, and traveled to 33 countries because my clients flew me all over the world. I was published in countless magazines. I got into a toxic marriage at 27. I moved to New York by 31 and was divorced by 32. Managed my business opportunities and did life on my own for the remaining years. By the time I got to Bali, I was exhausted. From the 19-hour flight, yes. But mostly from the years I'd spent trying to do everything by myself.

That young girl who jumped off the balance beam for the last time in Kansas City made a big decision. She would plunge ahead alone. I wouldn't rely on anyone for my dreams ever again just to have them taken from me. If I wanted something done, I had to do it myself. Lying on the yoga mat in Bali, I wasn't angry with her. I accepted that girl and the decision she made. *At a young age, you figured out a coping mechanism,* I said to myself. *Way to go. It helped you get through a lot of stuff. You were independent. You made a career for yourself. You sought travel. But . . .*

And this was a big *but.* The fact was that plunging ahead alone wasn't working for me anymore. It wasn't serving my life. The myth of self-sufficiency was an Anti-Belief that had been holding me back. Believing I had to do everything on my own didn't leave room for anybody else. I was energetically blocking other people from getting close to me. I could finally release that belief. I could surrender. I could let go of the Anti-Belief getting in the way of me manifesting the life I wanted.

It was a transcendent moment for me, and the peace I felt in that release was immense.

You might remember from the introduction how I had started my podcast in October 2019. I knew then that 2020 was going to be a big year. It had been going, going, going for me for a long time. The chaos of New York for two years. A divorce. Working constantly with no time to rest or heal.

As the days grew shorter during that fall, I had started imagining the tranquil jungles of Bali, with the gentle sound of rain falling on the leaves of coconut palm trees. On some deep spiritual level, I knew I had to get to the island that winter. A different time zone meant I would be free from phone calls and other interruptions. Plus, I had seen Julia Roberts ride her bike through the rice paddies in *Eat, Pray, Love* (Elizabeth Gilbert reaches into my life more than she knows), and I knew that was going to be a healing place for me to land.

I found a villa in Canggu on Airbnb that looked suitable as this would be my home for the next couple of months. On a practical level, I knew I had to get a visa and needed money. I had enough for the plane ticket but not for my stay.

I tried everything I could to bring in some quick cash, but nothing worked. Nobody was booking my photo shoots. By December, I still didn't have enough money for my stay at the villa, and I was getting close to canceling. I said, *Okay, universe, if this is something that is going to be transformative and healing for me, then provide the way for me to go. If not, then let things keep going in this direction. That will prompt me to cancel.* I said it was out of my hands, thinking that my trip wouldn't happen, but the universe had other plans.

I had recently become friends with a woman named Noelle. (Side note: she is now one of my best friends.) I lived across the street from this fancy bar she owned with her husband, and I had recently photographed her. Noelle loved the photographs and asked if I wanted to meet up for a Christmas brunch. We had gotten coffee a couple times, and I really liked her. I was all for this budding friendship. We sat down in this hotel restaurant that had great brunch but was completely empty because it was so close to Christmas. Noelle took a sip of her peppermint tea and said, "I got you something."

She handed me an envelope. I opened it, thinking it would be a holiday card, but, boy, was I wrong. It was a check for $1,000.

A thousand dollars? From the woman who owned the bar across the street from my house? A woman I'd photographed once and barely knew? I burst into tears.

"I know you're trying to go on this trip," she told me. "I felt led to give this to you."

This was insane. The means for making the trip had come through a virtual stranger. Scenes from *The Secret* flashed in my head—the scrolls, the torches, the Babylonians. I could hear Rhonda Byrne's Australian accent in my head. I had somehow been lucky enough to manifest this due to the generosity of my earth angel. As I tried to thank Noelle, she interrupted me and put her hand on my forearm and said, "If you need any more money while you're there, we'll take care of you."

Unbelievable, right?

I was shaking because I had this money in front of me, confronting a strong-held belief that I had to do everything by myself. This was staring me in the face, saying, *Actually, you don't. People love and care about your dreams and will even sacrifice their own money to help you see it through.* I was a puddle of tears.

But it happened. Thanks to that money from Noelle, I made it to the rice paddies and coconut palms of Bali while breaking down 20 years of extreme independence.

Halfway around the world, far from my family, I became good friends with a petite German girl who was staying in the same villa. And then we both became friends with a group of women, about 20 of us altogether. We hung out every day. We swam to the beach; we danced in the clubs. It was the epitome of sisterhood, the divine feminine. All of us were healing from broken relationships or scarring childhood experiences. We threw ourselves into ecstatic dance camps. We rode motorbikes out to waterfalls. We communed in worship ceremonies of self-love.

Some of the most magical experiences of my life took place in those jungles with that sisterhood. And some traumatic moments too. I was in a club one night and tried to help a girl we thought had been roofied. I tried to help her escape the grip of a persistent male who was dragging her around like a rag doll. I stood between them and broke their bond, and she ran for her life. I had only been in Bali for a couple days, but upon receiving a swift punch in the chest from a man, I quickly realized we were not in Kansas (City) anymore. So, it was not all rainbows and butterflies, but, nonetheless, we healed, we astral traveled, we awakened.

Which brings me back to the savasana pose. Remember, I was lying there in the courtyard on the floor and I had been asking myself, *Why can I not find love? Why is it so hard for me to find someone who sees me as beautiful? What is it about me that people don't want?*

Independent 12-year-old Alea was the answer to that question. I can't find love because life is all up to me. Just me. There was no space for anyone else to step in. I couldn't rely on anyone else for what I wanted, and thus I wasn't open energetically to that union I was looking for.

Recognizing this Anti-Belief was the first step. Next, I had to ask myself if it was true. Was it all up to me? I got to stay in Bali thanks to Noelle. The universe was telling me something. I had to let go of my myth of total self-reliance. For nearly two decades, I'd held on to it as my own "I don't need anyone" identity. But I wasn't in Bali totally on my own, which means I was already beginning to shift into a new reality. It was the trip that clarified my new reality. I lay on the mat, soaking in this new awareness.

You don't need to be that person anymore. You don't need that part of the narrative; you can let it go.

That was an incubation space that allowed me to have this revelation. If I believed people won't show up for me, then, guess what, they're not going to. Because even if they did, I wouldn't have seen it that way.

Letting that go meant letting other people in. Deep breaths. Some of the deepest breaths I'd ever taken. Change takes a lot of energy.

But holding on to an Anti-Belief takes energy too. And what's more, it's self-sabotage. In this case, I wanted romantic love, but I was keeping myself walled off from it. *I have to do everything myself. No one else can come in.* Well, there you have it. It's going to be hard to have an intimate relationship with those conditions.

Bringing attention to our Anti-Beliefs can be earth-shattering. It means saying good-bye to what our life has been built upon. It may not have been working for us, but it was still our life. Our comfort zone can be really uncomfortable, but we will choose it because it's the devil we know versus the devil we don't.

It's pretty big to wave good-bye to a whole way of being. When you ask if it has to be this way, if it is actually your reality, the answers can be tough to hear. We may resist them at first. So, yeah, I may have started this chapter describing a peaceful, transcendent moment on a yoga mat in a jungle in Southeast Asia, but that moment was a culmination of a lot of work. Untangling ourselves from Anti-Beliefs isn't easy, and the whole process is rarely peaceful.

It took me a long time to let go of the decision I made at age 12. And I still face Anti-Beliefs to this day. Sometimes the same one, sometimes another version. Recently, for example, I found myself in a space where I wasn't treating my body well because I didn't believe I deserved to be treated well, where I felt I didn't deserve to wear beautiful clothes. Why? More than one reason. Not all of them are consistent. When I was a kid, my mother felt shame around her body. She would never wear shorts, and I've never seen my mom in a swimsuit. I inherited that shame to a degree. Growing up Christian, that shame was compounded by the idea that my body was problematic for men. I'd want to wear something I liked but "I can't because that would mean I would be a stumbling block for my brothers in Christ." But, more importantly, "Even though I would like to wear certain things, it's better to blend in so I don't foster unwanted attention." I felt I needed to hide to stay safe. When I blossomed, I learned that there's such a thing as too much blossoming. From various directions, early on, I learned my body was problematic both for people I cared about and for people I did not care about. If I dressed in black, though, I could sort of hide from unwanted attention. So, that's how I dressed, often always in black.

As I was working on this chapter—still working on my Anti-Beliefs—I was getting ready to do a tent reading. I had this whole vintage circus theme going that needed extra flare. And guess what?

I said fuck it and decided I was going to wear red!

Even though I had spent my whole life avoiding that color, I looked incredible in that dress! I felt vibrant and empowered, and somehow putting on a different color changed the way I was able to see my body. It helped me inhabit a new point of view and gain distance from my

Anti-Belief that I didn't deserve to wear something so gorgeous. I don't think I'd have been able to feel good wearing this fabulous red dress if I hadn't dug into all the ways I had set limits around myself in terms of my body.

All this to say that after the massive face-to-face with my core Anti-Belief in Bali, I'm still working on myself for sure. My Anti-Beliefs aren't gone. But I'm coming to appreciate the lessons they contain when we examine them. They challenge what we want. The key is to identify them and challenge them. Duke it out. Ask: Is this real or just the story you're telling yourself? To do that, it helps to know where Anti-Beliefs come from. We'll get to that next.

The Origin of Anti-Beliefs

Where do Anti-Beliefs come from?

Glad you asked.

There is typically a wound at the root of these limiting beliefs. Perhaps to protect ourselves as children, we narrowed our view of the world. We let our sense of possibility shrink.

Let's try to access some of these limiting beliefs. First, think about what you want. Then, think about what obstacle rises up for you when you think about why you can't have it.

I want [x], but I can't have [x] because . . .

I want to be [x], but I can't be [x] because . . .

I want to do [x], but I can't do [x] because . . .

This is usually the first layer of where an Anti-Belief can exist. Another way to get at the core of the beliefs that challenge our desires is by asking how your Anti-Belief is serving you. What is it doing for you? Because, trust me, it's serving us in some way. Maybe it's keeping us safe from facing a fear, challenging the status quo; maybe it's keeping us from being more vulnerable or allowing us to stay in our comfort zone.

At the base of these Anti-Beliefs is usually something very thematic, and the core of our Anti-Beliefs is often the need for safety. The desire to minimize vulnerability. To keep ourselves from hoping. Which is strange, right? I'm guessing you love the idea of manifestation as much as I do, which is like hope activated. Hope on steroids. But then we hold on to something that keeps us from hoping. We stick with being comfortable in our discomfort. (The devil you know versus the devil you don't kind of thing, remember?)

Sometimes I think of it as holding on to our painful story. It can be almost pleasurable, can't it, to play the victim? We want to say: *See? I told you so. I told you I have to do everything around the house. I told you I had to stay at the job I don't like. I told you I'm stuck in this relationship. I told you no one would want to publish my book.* It's like we'd rather be right than happy. I may not have what I want, but at least I called it. And to some degree, it makes our ego feel better to massage those stories, comfort those stories, instead of tossing them into oblivion.

Now, what if someone has what they think is an Anti-Belief or limiting belief, but it's actually real? Like, if you ask how it's serving you, the answer is, it is keeping you grounded in reality. Let's take a simple example. What if, for example, I want to fly, but I have this belief that I can't fly? I don't mean fly in an airplane but jump off a cliff, spread my arms out, and soar through the clouds.

Well, that's not an Anti-Belief stopping you. As humans, we can't fly. I trust you have figured this out by now; like we mentioned before, gravity is a law, so there is no way around this one. That manifestation (without any kind of tech assisting you in flight) just won't come true. Whatever you are facing is probably a little more complex than that, but there may be times when what you're telling yourself is stopping you is the truth. Maybe you don't have the money to quit your job. Maybe you can't move to another country because of visa requirements and closed borders. Then again, maybe you can. Don't give up before you interrogate that Anti-Belief to make sure that it's not just a story.

When I was dating in NYC, the Anti-Belief was that I want to be in an equal and capable partnership, but no one wanted to date me because I'm a black plus-size woman, and people only want white girls. To my experience, all my petite white girlfriends had men in their lives that wanted to commit to them, and I only had men that treated me as if I was disposable. That was the experience I had within my view of the Anti-Belief I was holding. I always felt overlooked. While that was partially true, when I go back to whom I was dating, there were guys who wanted to hang out more, who wanted a second or third date or that were really kind and nice, and I didn't notice them because my story was that no one wanted me, and I couldn't break that story's character arc.

When I finally recognized what I was doing, it was a game changer, y'all. I was no longer left out of my own story.

Try This

Is there an Anti-Belief holding you back from getting what you want? If so, what is it? Let's bring it out into the light and examine it. Let's vet and audit each one. Let's not let anything slip by, accepted as true when it may not be.

If there is more than one, take them one by one. State the belief. Maybe even write it down. Now, think about it. Is it true? We have to ask the following questions:

Is this true, or is this the story I'm telling myself?

If it feels true, ask further questions: Why is that the truth for me? What has caused me up to this point to believe this to be true?

Does this story keep me protected?

Does it keep me from being vulnerable and getting disappointed?

How does this story serve me?

This might be a good time to let you in on something kind of fun. If you pay attention, you'll see the universe giving you hints that your Anti-Belief is not true. (If it's not true. If it's like the flying one and it is true, then hold on to it.) Lots of times we block out anything that goes against our Anti-Belief. But if we start letting ourselves crack the walls of that block, we will start receiving new messages that could change our lives forever.

If you're trying to manifest, you better learn how to receive, so you might as well start practicing. You're going to get offers all the time from this beautiful universe of ours. But you're not going to see what's happening right in front of you if you don't know how to accept it.

Do You Have to Do Everything?

One Anti-Belief that comes up consistently in conversations with my clients is a version of the one I began telling myself at age 12. In short, some variation on the idea that "I have to do everything. It's all up to me."

Do you feel like this is true in your life?

If you do, I have another question for you. (I have a lot of questions.)

Do you ever ask anyone for help?

Often, when I pursue this follow-up question with my clients, they say no, they don't ask anyone for help. They're waiting for someone to offer. And it turns out even when someone offers, many of them say, "No thanks."

So, if that's the case, the first step is probably obvious. Accept help next time someone offers. (And then you can find out if you're willing to relinquish control enough to let someone help.)

But let's say it's true that no one is offering to help. Then you might ask: Why is it that people don't see me as someone who has needs? Is that something I want? Do I want to be seen as someone who needs help? Have I taken the time to express my needs to others? Do I believe I am worthy of help? Do I believe others are capable of the help I need, of the kind of help that would actually help?

Even in my household now, there are times where I feel I have to do everything. Yet I have a husband who does more than any husband I've ever seen. He cleans first thing in the morning and washes all the dishes. What the f*ck am I complaining about? I think part of me in my feminine energy really wants to be able to be a stay-at-home mom without work on the side. Not have to figure stuff out. But I know I would not be happy that way, and in fact the universe gave me a stint of being able to feel what that felt like. I was out of work over the holidays and for months was unable to contribute to our household finances. My husband did it all: worked, paid all the bills, and still helped get the kids to school, cleaned, and helped me with every new house project I came up with. (I'm a very lucky woman.)

So, then, why do I have this feeling? I think it arises when I feel isolated because I am overwhelmed. It's an imprinted mindset from my past and my comfortable narrative that arises on days I wish to pooh-pooh on my life. But on days I'm able to recognize the truth and not lose myself in the enchantment of the story I'm telling myself, I understand that I'm returning to childhood. To what is most primal.

In those deregulated moments, I am returning to this idea that I need to parent myself and be the one to anticipate danger. Back to the Anti-Belief I identified in the savasana pose. Yes, so much comes back to that core. *It's up to me. Everything hinges on me.* That's how I interpreted things as a child at a formative time. That was the belief I latched onto and based my identity around. Turns out I can't get rid of it entirely after one outstanding yoga session.

That core meant feeling lonely and scared. It followed me for a really long time, and sometimes it still rears its head. And each time it does, I'm given the chance to release that Anti-Belief again and shift my focus toward a new one. A belief that serves me better. *It's not all up to me. Others are supporting me. Others are helping me. I'm part of a collective. We are lifting each other up.*

Those moments when we regress to an earlier version of ourselves can be painful, but they present an opportunity. They give us a choice. Are we that earlier version of ourselves, or are we a new version? Are we reacting to something we've been wounded by? Can we be gentle with that earlier self, the one who felt wounded? Can we recognize this moment as a chance to heal?

Give Yourself Time and Space

Give yourself time to work through your Anti-Beliefs and the questions that arise. Sit with the questions. Sit with the answers. Allow yourself space.

I know it's not easy to do. The speed of our lives doesn't make it easy to sit with anything. We can't sit, period. We have to run. We're behind. We're missing out. We have FOMO. Patriarchal and capitalist forces push us along at an unsustainable rate. We need to make x amount of money by such and such age. Buy a house. Save up enough money for our kids to go to college. Wait, are we going to have kids? Not much time to think about that either. We need to consume and consume and consume. We're not enough. We don't have enough. We always need more.

This work of Meaningful Manifestation runs counter to the patriarchal capitalist forces pushing us to rush along and consume. It takes guts to overcome these forces and make time for a practice of self-reflection and to welcome a pause for self-awareness and spend time asking the self, *What do I believe? Why do I believe that?* Given everything else going on in our lives, this path can feel like a bit of a detour. But it's the essential work we have to do. Eventually, we will be given the opportunity to make a choice, because we will come to see the choice we had ruled out is actually available to us. Meaningful Manifestation is about agency. It's about accepting our power. Wearing our red dress.

And that's a little scary, right?

The safest thing we can do is *not* give this work the time it needs in the first place. We can stay hidden and offstage by telling ourselves, in fact, that we don't have time. *What's the thing I want? I can't have it. It's out of reach. It's off limits. That job, that boyfriend, that vacation, that sense of security, that lifestyle—not an option for me.* There is pain in waiting, there is also pain in hoping. We worry, *What if what I hope for doesn't come true?* But what if it does? It requires us to step outside of our comfort in this microwave culture and be open to possibilities we have maybe never seen before. We often end up shutting something down before we give it its proper time to flourish.

If I *can't* have something, I don't have to be vulnerable to wanting it. If I don't hope, I don't have to be disappointed. In a paradoxical way, the painful story of our Anti-Belief keeps us from taking any risks.

Most of us go through our lives not aware we are fighting with ourselves over something we could have, but maybe can't have right now.

I don't look good in red. I'm not safe in my body. I need to hide, I told myself for years. Except I do look good in red. I am safe. And I don't need to hide.

I'm unlovable, and no one will ever find me attractive. I'll end up settling just to have someone commit to me. Except that I am lovable and didn't have to settle at all. I hit the jackpot!

I'm a terrible writer, and no one will ever be interested in what I have to say. Except that 10 million downloads on my podcast would say otherwise.

More questions for you. What is your version of wearing red? Can you do it today? With gusto? With a sense of adventure? What's stopping you?

Never let a narrative have this much power over you.

Chapter 7

Growth

What Change Needs to Happen to Get It

Transformation.
I think I've used the word close to 10 times in this book already. And now we are at the step in the IMAGINE process where it's going to begin to happen. In the following pages, we will give ourselves time for more imagining. We'll continue listening to our intuition. We'll embrace more spiritual (and a fair amount of psychological) shit.

This chapter is going to ask a lot of you. We're going to be creating space for reframing beliefs, writing bold new narratives, and making shifts to empower ourselves. This is not sitting back and letting the manifestation happen. There is a place for that receptive mode—in fact we'll talk about the power of surrender in the following chapter, Integration. But here we're going to come face-to-face with what you need to change, and, if you're not willing to change, we will try to find out why. Either way, are you ready to grow as a person? Let's jump in!

The work we'll do here will bring you deeper into knowing who you are and deeper into trusting yourself. You have already given some thought to what makes a good life for you and what is most important to you (your Maxims for a Good Life). You've determined your Inception Point and have a clearer idea now about what it is you actually want to Manifest. Plus, you've done the hard work of exploring your Anti-Beliefs.

Now you are ready for *G*, Growth! Growth means change. Think of nature—growth can't happen without something shifting, often dramatically. When a joyful field of sunflowers starts to wilt and die in late summer, the flowers lose their petals. Only then are the seeds ready to fly off and begin again. And the roots can only start growing when the seed cracks open.

It's fun to talk about sunflowers because they are associated with positive energy as well as spiritual growth. Native Americans found all kinds of health benefits in them, and many artists and poets have been inspired by them as well. But now let's seize that vibrant energy, and turn to *you*. What change needs to happen for you to transform like the sunflower seeds? The change itself is what we call the Growth Point.

The growth that needs to happen is often big, but many times the steps you need to take are small. Something isn't working anymore for you, and it's keeping you from moving forward. Sometimes you need a belief to be extracted and replaced with a new one.

Everything always falls to me. I need to become more comfortable asking others for help.

I don't have time to exercise because of a demanding career. I can make time for a daily walk by cutting out social media scrolling.

I can't join a band because I'm not good at music. I can start practicing guitar 10 minutes a day following a YouTube video.

When we face this moment, the Growth Point, we may start to observe pain and often fear. It's pretty hard to face pain and fear head-on, but I hope you can be present in this task. We *want* to confront this discomfort. That is how we grow. By facing the discomfort, acknowledging it, accepting it, and allowing it, we can ask ourselves what we want to do about it. We can think deeply about our patterns of behaviors and our habits and decide which of them we want to change.

This part of the process is about sitting down and looking at the pain point, then asking yourself how you want to overcome this. I've talked quite a bit about my health journey, so let's look at where the Growth Point would be in that context.

The Growth Point: A New Health Regimen

To manifest the body I want, I've determined that I need to get up at 5:30 A.M. to take the pills that are part of my health regimen and to get myself to the gym. There would be lots of chia seeds and apple cider vinegar. My Anti-Belief (one of them) is that I don't have time—*Three kids! A book to write! A revamped podcast! Medium readings!* But in spite of real scheduling challenges, that is a story I'm telling myself that I don't have the time. I actually *do* have time for a workout, if I get up early enough.

My Inception Point is the state of my health before starting this routine, and the Manifestation Point is where I want to be in terms of my health.

One day after starting this new regimen, I realized I wasn't going to the gym anymore. I didn't stay faithful to my goals. I was so tired in the mornings, my kid is still waking up sometimes during the night, and I'm a horrible sleeper. But I was still guilting myself around this goal I had made. "See, you have no discipline." The Anti-Belief crept in. So, where is the accountability? That's the Growth Point. That is where the pain and the fear I warned you about may begin to creep in.

Well, okay, let's look more closely at the situation. I do have some physical hurdles (a young child, a hormone disorder) that make it difficult to achieve the body I want to achieve. And I also have a mental block: that health is only about the size I am, not the state of my rest, the quality of the food I eat, my mental wellness, and how strong or mobile I am. And sometimes maybe I want to sit on the couch and eat a bowl of cereal in the morning. The only way I thought I could make progress is to stay hypervigilant all day, starting with the 5:30 A.M. wake up and gym routine. It requires a hell of a lot of energy. While I do have a lot of energy, I also have a lot of things I need to do with that energy on any given day.

Plus, there is a homeostasis where my body feels comfortable. Right now, I am not willing to get up and push past the comfort of this homeostasis and go to the gym day after day. Is my desire to be in better health stronger than my desire to be comfortable? If I want to manifest that Health Point, then I would have to abandon what is comfortable. Is there a wound I need to look at? Probably. Is staying at my current weight serving me in some way? Yes. I wouldn't continue on this path unless it served me in some way. Maybe this weight protects my energy, keeps me more grounded, and shelters me from absorbing all the crap others put out. Not going to the gym is serving me because I can be a hermit. Maybe what I really want to do is conserve my energy, not lose 50 pounds.

Yet another variable here is that my medium work leaves me energetically drained. It is a job that requires me to take on other people's pain. That means I don't have energy to give myself to manifest the body I want. In fact there is a direct correlation between how many sessions I do and how much weight I gain. Most days I'm so depleted, I can't give attention to one of my Maxims, my health.

But here is yet another discovery that's useful. I work and work and work to make the money I need to feel safe. That drains the energy I would need to do a healthy workout, but my safety is a higher priority for me than my health. That means that financial security is a higher Maxim than my health. However, the way I am operating now is causing me to harm a lower Maxim and push it even further down. One option here could be to go back and revise my Maxims if I so choose to believe that health is a higher Maxim than money (which for me it is).

And there's yet another way that my current routine of sleeping past 5:30 A.M. and missing my time slot for the gym serves me. It gratifies my ego. *See? It's impossible to fit everything into my day. See? I'll never be a fashion-model size. I told you—it's out of my control.* I have to interject here because why was a fashion-model size my definition of health? There are plenty of skinny people teeming with health issues. When did I decide that being smaller would be a Maxim? And why did I decide that 5:30 A.M. for a new mom was the goal during the most brutal time to get up during the winter? It's like I was setting myself up to fail.

If I sabotage myself, I can predict the outcome—I'm not going to lose weight. I'm not going to reach that predefined Health Point, so maybe it's time I refine what health means to me instead of abiding by what society has tried to force me to fit into. Additionally, I can tell myself that I'm not loved and accepted as I am. If I weighed less, then I'd be more loved. If all these conditions were met, then I'd be okay. And this is just not true! It's just the story I'm telling myself and have been telling myself for a long time because that also means I don't have to be vulnerable to the possibility that I work really hard and still don't end up fitting into the size 12 jeans I have waiting in the closet. *Fuck those jeans!* They can't taunt me. They can't hurt me. I don't even *want* to fit into them.

Do I want to be a smaller size? Why do I want to be a smaller size? What have been the prevailing messages that I have been flooded with since I was a child? And how did I go from having a 12-year eating disorder, extreme body dysmorphia, to not feeling safe in my body anymore? Have I ever felt safe in my own body?

Wow. (If you haven't caught on, this is where we see growth.)

Asking myself these questions started to get to the root of where my weight issues come from.

Trigger warning: I'm about to tell a story about sexual assault.

When I was 18, I was essentially kidnapped by an upperclassman from my college. The short version is a big group of students decided we were all going to go to the movies together. There was a guy, we will call him Eric, who had been trying to get me to go on a date with him. He was a senior and the star of the football team. I had no interest in him at all because he thought he was some big shot, and I was not impressed. So, as we were all getting ready to go out, we were trying to figure out whose cars we would be riding in. I didn't have my own car, so he suggested that I ride with him, but I declined. When my girlfriends didn't have space left in their cars, he was the only option. After some pressure I said, "Okay, but we are just going as friends, not a date." He agreed, "Yes, just as friends." I got in the car, and the drive took longer than expected. Now, remember, we didn't have smartphones with GPS back then, but we arrived at the theater, and I kept calling the other friends to see where they were. If you haven't guessed by now, he took me to a different theater way outside of town.

I wanted to leave immediately, but he insisted we go see the movie since we already bought the tickets. "He had tickets for the wrong theater?" No, he had tickets for that theater because this was his plan all along. And the next two hours felt like the most traumatic game of keep-away. I was touched in places I shouldn't have been. I got up and changed seats to get away from him and tried to "play it cool" so he wouldn't leave me there with no way to get home. Eric told me that if I didn't kiss him, he would leave me there. I had just turned 18; he was 23.

He attempted to take me back to his place, but I told him that my R.A. was expecting me back at the dorm because we were having a meeting, and she would know that I was gone and come looking for me. It was just enough of a lie for him to drop me off. The next day, rumors had been floating around that we went "all the way." That was clearly a lie, but it made me feel absolutely sick. I went into the cafeteria and ate three of those big 10-inch Belgian waffles.

This was a formidable moment in my life that told me, "I am not safe in a body men find attractive." So, I gained the freshman 15 and then some. I replaced my eating disorder with another one. I didn't think this consciously but as a coping mechanism to my trauma. I remembered that when I was a chunky middle schooler, no one noticed me, so I would become invisible again.

I've recently been working through all those questions we mentioned earlier about the idea of sabotage and why when I start to see progress, I abandon ship. Well, through this method I use in my own life, I found the belief that was deeper than my health Maxim, which was safety. I sat in a meditation and what came out shocked me: my fear of bad attention from men is higher than my fear of death due to bad health.

I was eating to stay alive, to stay safe, and every time I would start to lose weight or find consistency in an exercise routine, fears I had suppressed when I was 18 would start to arise. Never with the conscious message that would help me understand why but with an alarming blockade that wouldn't allow me to get to my goal because my goal interfered with my safety.

I'm crying my eyes out right now as I'm typing this. It's a type of freedom I haven't felt in a long time. Freedom from all the shame and guilt I've been putting on myself for not being disciplined enough. Hate for a body that's only wanted to keep me safe, and a real chance to dig deep at the root of what's been oppressing me for so long. The mixed signals of wanting to be attractive, to be loved, but also wanting to be invisible to stay safe.

For years, I didn't think about this incident, but when I did, I always pictured him with a different face. Writing this book triggered me to realize that I was dissociating, and my body felt I was ready to see his real face. My trauma protected me for a long time, but I was ready to face him. When my brain allowed me to integrate, I saw the sick little face of my abuser after 22 years, and it triggered a panic attack. But I used every bit of courage to sit with my discomfort and write a new story about my body.

It started with me saying to myself, *Health has always been focused on size and being smaller. Society tells women that small is more attractive so that we will be frail and easy to overpower. What if the compromise to my experience and my health is to become stronger? Maybe health is self-defense classes, strengthening muscles and mobility, building muscle, and not being so focused on size but strength.*

Now that's a Maxim I can get on board with.

I will never do cardio (unless it's fun) again. I will lift weights and do strength training that will make me feel strong. I currently can leg-press 550 pounds, and the guys at the gym are always skeptical when they see me putting on so much weight but jaws drop when they see I can press it 10 times. And that's given a whole new meaning to thunder thighs, my friends. Those legs aren't squeezing into size 12 jeans, and I'm finally okay with that. I feel strong and being able to cultivate and refine my ask for my health Maxim has felt so empowering and is something I can actually stick with. But I couldn't have done that if I wasn't able to be vulnerable.

I had to ask myself what if the work of loving myself and feeling confident has nothing at all to do with my weight and everything to do with ME: my past, my family, my heart, my trauma, my intuition, my willingness to be vulnerable, and my willingness to be alive and thriving?

Maybe I'll discover that now is not the time for me to lose weight. And if that's the case, then I can stop guilting myself over it. I can stop looking at clothes that don't fit. What if I'm okay and love my body exactly as it is and what it's done for me to stay alive?

No change.

No shame.

No guilt.

Would I be happier? Maybe. I could explore that. Being excluded from fashion is not fun. I like fashion. I'm creative. I enjoy artistic expression of clothing. What always makes me feel so shitty is when I go into the store and they don't have my size. That happens all the time. So, is this weight limiting my creative expression, or is that just the story I'm telling myself?

I hope the above demonstrates that the Growth Point requires willingness to engage in a fair amount of introspection and digging through the mess of our traumas. It's not a straight path. It's more like a spirited debate and brainstorm with yourself. Allow any thought to come into the picture. Consider as many angles as possible. Don't settle on any one conclusion too soon or you'll miss the opportunity for exploration and healing.

Yes, getting up and out to the gym is, for most people, hard. Yes, some things in my life are unique to this moment and body that make it particularly hard. But if I'm going to grow, I can't just end the internal conversation there. And trust me, I'd love to leave it there. It doesn't require me to face myself or dig into my wounds. I can stay comfortable in my discomfort. It's familiar. (See the sidebar The Comfort of Familiarity.) But this is the Meaningful Manifestation we are after. And that can only come when we're willing to do the work.

This leads us back to vulnerability. It takes effort to have the vulnerability to hope for the thing I want. I might fail a bunch of times. I might struggle, I might need to reroute, redefine. I will devote energy. Possibly I'll embarrass myself. I'll make some progress; and it will fall away. Right now, I'm thinking I've got to stop swinging in extremes. As long as I'm moving my body, I'm not going to shame myself. All that shaming does is take me further from my goal.

This health journey—this is a major one for me. I'm still working on how to reframe my beliefs and where this should go in my Maxims. This Growth Point is related to a bad wound that I have, and it will take more digging to sort out. It might be a lifelong process getting in contact through these questions to what blocks me.

Once I see that's happening, again I have choices. Am I going to let health slip right off my Maxims for a Good Life? Or will I make adjustments to how I treat myself, talk to myself, and support my physical self? Do I need to rear-range how I think about health so that it is consistent with what health and wellness actually mean for me to live a good life according to my Maxims?

No one at my funeral is going to think about what I weighed on the scale. So, what about my weight will have determined whether or not I lived a good life? In fact, con-stantly trying to lose weight made my life a living hell! Yes, I want to be healthy, but I had to redefine what healthy meant to me. Maybe I weigh 200 pounds because I'm sheer fucking muscle. I used to live and die by the scale, even though it was never an indicator on my actual health.

All the questions and exploration can start to feel over-whelming. But what I've learned is, I can take it day by day. I've manifested careers, a romantic partner, a family, a pod-cast, a book, and so much more. But that doesn't mean I am done and have it all figured out. I'm still very much in this process with you.

You might be manifesting abundantly, or you might also have a Growth Point where you can spend years dig-ging and still not get to the point of Integration. I don't expect you to work through the prompts in this book, solve a lifelong wound, and get on with things by the last page. I'm just hoping to give you a structure for gaining more insight into what you want to bring into your life and to appreciating all that you already have.

The answers to the questions I'm posing will change over time. Our behaviors will certainly change over time. At least if we can begin by asking the right questions and figuring out how much of what happens in our lives is actually under our control, we'll have a greater chance of success. Maybe what you need to bring in is more patience and self-awareness. Those two things might be the healing in any given space. They'll serve you well, no matter what direction you choose.

If you feel you are caught in a holding pattern, ask yourself if you're staying somewhere (metaphorically) because it is serving you somehow.

In what way is it serving you?

Is it comfortable?

Is it comforting to be able to predict the outcome?

Is it gratifying your ego?

Is it trying to keep you safe from something?

Take time to explore. Gather what you can from your experiences and learn as much as you can from them. You'll notice from everything I've written about the Growth Point of my health journey that I haven't yet settled on one direction in this space. I'm not committing to those pre-sunrise mornings yet. Instead, I've asked myself a lot of questions, and posited some answers. The Growth Point was an opening. It is where I said to myself: *This is what needs to happen, and if I'm not doing it, why not? Where am I accountable, and where can I flip the premise and consider it from another angle? I have insane muscle mass. I am keeping up with my toddler. I'm showing up for work and family, so who says this isn't exactly where I'm meant to be?*

Growth is messy. It can't happen without dramatic change and often loss.

Digging in your heart and through your past is like digging in the garden: it's going to get your hands extremely dirty. I've said all along the work we do is about healing and growing and knowing ourselves better. If you're facing your pain and your fears, you're learning and growing, and that is the entire goal of the Growth Point.

The Comfort of Familiarity

As I wrote in the Introduction, we human beings often find change hard. We are used to a certain way of being. We are comfortable with what is familiar, even when the familiar is feeling constantly overscheduled, or being unhappy with our living space, or dating people who are not supportive. Maybe the familiar is getting into a fight every holiday. Whatever it is, we may be comfortable in this discomfort. It's a bit of a paradox. But let's think through why this might be the case.

Why is an uncomfortable position comfortable? It's what you know. You know what to say. You know what to do. You follow the patterns that are already established. It's like a script you've already memorized. It takes effort to depart from the familiar. It takes effort to change our routine, to change how we think. Growth is not easy! We actually have to rewrite our neural pathways to start going in a different direction.

My husband, David, sometimes has a difficult time relaxing. One day in summer, I suggested we take a trip to the beach. "What am I going to do there?" he asked, looking a bit anxious already. "Relax," I tell him. You want to know his reply? "That sounds stressful!"

As a kid, David never had a moment where he could slack off. There was always something he had to do. If his mom sensed that he wasn't being productive in some way, she would find something for him to do. He is programmed to just keep checking off task after task. It takes effort to change the programming. So, even though relaxing should be . . . well, relaxing . . . it's not to him. It can at times cause him anxiety. Not relaxing is what is familiar.

And David is not all that unique in this trait. Relaxing is not relaxing to many people. So many people are workaholics by choice. Many of us fill our calendars to within an inch of our lives, by choice. Many of us run from one thing to the next, with barely time to catch our breath from one activity before the next one begins.

Relaxing means being quiet with our thoughts, having to think about the things we might not want to think about, and dealing with things you might have been avoiding. None of this is easy. All those things invite vulnerability. All of them move us away from the comfortable perch of the safe and familiar to the treacherous and uncertain.

Trust Yourself

Now let's turn to you. Let's pick one thing you want to manifest. You can pick something you've already identified in a previous chapter of this book. This is your goal. Take out your journal, phone, or notebook and answer these questions as honestly as you can:

What are you doing to achieve this goal?

If you're not doing what needs to be done, is it because you're attached to something else? To comfort? To a familiar pattern? To a certain type of person you've always dated or friendship you've always had?

Where can you take accountability?

Is there a wound you need to look at?

Energetically speaking, what are you used to in this space?

Why might you be resisting change?

What are you willing to let go of?

Letting go is an important part of this process as well. It might be the you who gets to sleep in until at least sunrise. It might be the you who doesn't have to travel around promoting your book and worrying about whether enough people will show up to hear you read. It might be the you who gets to eat whatever you want for dinner every night because you only have to worry about you!

By letting go, you're inviting in a new reality, a life you love. You need to make space for it.

Let's imagine what it will feel like when we start to allow our psychological response to open up to something new. And first, let's acknowledge that, as uncomfortable as we may be now, changing is also going to cause some discomfort.

What Are You Really Seeking?

Now I want to try a little experiment. Let's take the goal you wrote about above and dig a little further into what may be behind it. Whether you want to run a marathon, land a part in a play, or improve your relationship with your mother-in-law, let's think about what you're *actually* seeking.

What do I mean by *actually seeking*? Well, if you want to run a marathon, is it because you want to prove to someone (or yourself) that you can? Is it a way to motivate yourself to exercise? Is it a focus on cardiovascular fitness after a worrying checkup? Is it because your friend is running, and you want to have this shared experience? Are you running in memory of someone to raise money for a cause dear to your heart? What's underneath the desire to run the marathon? What does it represent to you?

Here is another example. If you dream about spending a few weeks of summer in France, are you hoping to learn a new language? Do you want to escape your current routine? Are you looking for adventure? Are you interested in the landscape, the temples, the history? Are you studying to be a pastry chef? Are you entranced by the Mediterranean Sea? Perhaps it's the food or a love of movies. When you get closer to what it is you're looking for—what the idea of the trip represents—then you can evaluate whether a summer in France is the best way to find it. Does the trip in fact align with your Maxims? If not, do you want to revise your Maxims or perhaps consider another way to spend summer break?

Keep asking. Keep digging. If you want to learn a new language, why? Is it because you've "always wanted to"? Why have you always wanted to? Will it enhance your research? Look good on your résumé? Do you love the sound of it? Do you envy people who speak a second language? Do you want to read the poetry of romantic fictional love stories in the original French? With every answer, you can ask another why.

By embracing this exploration into the why behind our desires, we can often introduce a flexibility *to* our desires. Introducing flexibility will help us learn how to better target the driving desire underneath and bring them closer into the realm of reality.

Let me take this opportunity to tell you about a client of mine—we'll call her Sara—who was willing to do this work into the why behind her desire. Sara wanted to find a man, but she never seemed to have any luck. She thought she was too old and maybe something was wrong with her. By going through each step of the IMAGINE method, she first uncovered her Anti-Belief, that maybe this just wasn't in the cards for her. She accepted that that was a story she was telling herself. But going further into the exploration I've outlined above, Sara found out her actual issue is that she had determined at an earlier age that she never wants to rely on a man to survive. This core conviction was different from her Anti-Belief.

Digging further, Sara uncovered her difficult childhood. She had grown up watching her mother be dependent on a controlling husband. He pulled all the purse strings, and even though her mom wanted to leave, she believed she couldn't because she had no way of supporting herself. Sometime in early childhood, Sara decided that she would "never have to rely on a man," and so she didn't. She became a successful lawyer and worked really hard to have her own practice. Despite all her success, she never had a meaningful relationship. "Maybe men are intimidated by you," her friends tried to offer. But, if she was trying to manifest a man that wasn't . . . where the hell was he? Well, news flash, being part of a loving relationship does require a certain amount of relying on one another. It doesn't mean relying on someone unreliable, but it does mean opening yourself up to someone else and allowing yourself to depend on them relationally.

It turned out that Sara's perspective—based on the wound of her past—was keeping her single. She was literally not *letting* any man get close to her, hence the reason she couldn't find anyone. Now she had her Growth Point. Was she ready to change and rid herself of this refusal to let anyone in? Can she abandon her comfortable script? Can she let go of the ego gratification of saying, *I told you so! A relationship just isn't in the cards for me?* Can Sara give up the way she is being served by this wall of protection she's built? Can she open herself to romance? Can she experience the awakening required for that romance to happen?

Where can she take accountability?

Why might she be resisting change?

What is she willing to let go of to allow romance to enter?

Ask yourself the same questions. IMAGINE your way forward.

The Comfort of Self-Sabotage

We've talked a bit about the comfort we find in familiarity. There's an even more pernicious kind of comfort, and that is the comfort in self-sabotage. People like to identify with their struggles. And it feels good to be able to predict the outcome. To say, *See? He didn't like me.* The ego takes it less harshly. It's even a bit of a boost. *I was right!* Who doesn't like to be right?

See? I was right—I couldn't write a book.

See? I was right—I couldn't run a 5K.

See? I was right—I'm stuck in this town with no career prospects.

See? I was right—No one likes me. I'll be single forever.

I'm right. I'm safe. I have control. I know what to do next. I know what to say next.

Speaking of writing a book, I wanted to write a book. So bad! I wrote two. I made vision boards showing myself at a book signing. I even had a picture of Oprah on there. I was going to be on Oprah with my book. But it didn't happen. The books went nowhere. They both flopped.

See? I'll never be an author!

I could have gotten myself stuck to that idea. I could have wallowed in the gratification of giving up. It's just not going to happen for me. I could have held on to that belief. Who says I can't retreat to the safety of a smaller life? But instead, I took the steps to align myself with who I am at this stage, where I am better positioned to write *this* book. I studied, I interviewed experts, I moved ahead with my podcast. The social media landscape changed, and, as I've written about in this book already, an editor sent me a message. I could have been steeped in my despair and not paid attention to the message. *Oh, that must be a scam,* I could have said, dismissing it because I'll never be an author. Remember?

But here I am.

I didn't wallow in that self-gratification of knowing the outcome. Or stay with the comfort of the familiar. *I'm good at podcasting—I'll stick with that.* Instead, I let the outcome come to me. *Universe, what will you have for me?*

Holding On to Your Authentic Desires

Some of the exploration you do in this chapter will lead you back to the work we did in Chapter 3, Determine Your Maxims for a Good Life, where I asked you to vet your desires. We face all kinds of external pressures—*we're not good enough, we haven't done enough, we could be bettering ourselves, we're not making enough money.* It's hard not to compare ourselves to other people. Sometimes we want to achieve something to compensate for a lack of self-worth. Society says you're missing out if you don't do X. But wait—do you want to do X? Maybe we are spurred on by something we see on social media. And then there are real environmental factors putting pressure on our lives—mental health and social structures are indeed failing us as citizens.

All this to say it's important to recognize that we are all facing external pressure, some of it unavoidable and some of it we put on ourselves by spending too much time scrolling social media, for example. What we have to hold on to as we navigate these forces is that we don't need the best or perfect life. We just need a good life, which brings us back to Chapter 1. When we act in response to external pressures, we never get to a place where we can rest and enjoy the life we have. It's always, "What's next?"

The ultimate "what's next" experience came for me back when I was a wedding photographer.

In that role, it was important to me to be the *best*. I wanted to reach the top. And I got there. I was featured in top magazines. I did a couple really big covers. But despite these major successes, it never felt like enough. It was always go, go, go. I felt like I couldn't take a moment to rest and enjoy my successes because I had to keep fighting to keep myself at the top. You had to be *crushing* it. I would fly to Hong Kong for a bridal campaign. Paris. Milan. Portland. California.

As soon as I wrapped, I felt like people would ask, "What's your next project?" It had to be bigger, grander, more *wow* than the last one. People thought I was killing it. One summer, I went to nine different cities in six weeks. But guess what happens when you go, go, go like that? You burn out.

Maybe I was at the top (whatever that means). But I was also *tired*. My schedule exhausted me. *Looking* at my schedule exhausted me. I was traveling alone. I was stressed. It was fun, but it was not at a level that was safe for my mental health. Even doing the big covers had lost its shine. Keeping myself at that level wasn't sustainable. What was I looking for, and was I going to find it by running and running and running all over the world? I had to ask myself what I was seeking in this nonstop bid to stay on top.

What was I really seeking?

Stepping down from that peak in itself was growth. That took quieting all the external noise and listening to my own voice. That meant even listening to what I wanted to create, instead of taking whatever was given to me. I could be more selective. For years, I had chased that career, and I got to the top. Did I enjoy it? It was lovely up there for a while, but the truth was, the schedule didn't give me time to enjoy the view. And it didn't give me a chance to find a romantic partner, let alone put time into my health, let alone start a family. Not when I was always booked on the next flight out of town. I was booking my calendar full based on survival—social survival, financial survival, and self-esteem survival. It was time to change all that.

What If You're Not Ready to Change?

Okay, what if you've opened yourself up, you've faced your pain and your fears, and you've decided you want to back away from this Growth Point? (Even though, as I've argued above, you've already grown a lot just through this process.) If you are not ready to change, then let's think more about how *not* changing is serving you.

Is it keeping you safe?

Is it keeping you comfortable?

Is it boosting your ego?

Is it keeping you from being vulnerable?

When you come to a clearer understanding of how your resistance is serving you, you'll be in a better position to determine if you really want to change, or if you want to stay where you are for now. When something hasn't come into your life that you've called in, do you confront your beliefs about why? Why does it feel that opportunity is not available? In the next chapter, we will talk about what action to take when you've decided you're not ready for a change.

Let's go through a few more quick examples of how the Growth Point pushes us to know ourselves better, and, hopefully, ultimately to heal.

Rose is a woman in her late 20s who lives just north of San Francisco. Rose enjoys her job at a talent agency and has a few close friends with whom she enjoys hiking and going to see art films downtown. But one thought consumes Rose day and night—she wants to be a mother. She cannot stop scrolling Instagram accounts of moms frolicking with their toddlers. She's even taken to stopping in a children's clothing store in Presidio Heights on the way home from work. Let's find out more about what's behind her desire with a few questions.

Q: What is the thing you want to manifest?
Rose: I want to have a family.

Q: What does that mean to you? What does the experience look like? (Also, a hidden, but important part of this line of inquiry: What wounds are you trying to pacify?)
Rose: Someone to love me unconditionally.

Q: What if your kid decides they hate you? Will you still feel like the thing you asked for was a manifestation that you wanted?
Rose: Well, my kid wouldn't hate me. I would be a really good mom. [In protest as we do when we want something really bad and don't want to face such extreme opposition.]

Q: Having a child means sleeping less and taking on an enormous amount of stress. Are you ready to invite less sleep and more stress into your life?
Rose: I hadn't thought about that part, but yes . . . maybe?

Q: Are you willing to give up your time, your resources, and even your career path to make way for this little being?
Rose: I mean yes, but that seems really difficult to contend with on my own.

Q: Have you considered where you live regionally and the world circumstances to determine if now is a good time to bring a child into the world?

Rose: Well, no, I hadn't thought about that, but who thinks about that?

Q: Do you have enough financial and emotional support to help with raising the child?
Rose: Not the financially just yet, but I'm working on it. I have family here that would help me out, I think.

Q: Is the motivation for having a child for the child to have a good life or for you?
(crickets)

Children don't get to choose to be born, so often we are bringing souls in for a motivation or even an expectation that is wholly our own. That can be tough when the child doesn't abide by those expectations and when we are unaware of the real implications of what we are asking for.

We've given Rose a lot to think about here, to evaluate the good and sometimes the not-so-good of the things that we are asking for.

Now let's turn to Alan. Alan wants to be a millionaire. He's been working at a decent job in data analytics for about 10 years. He makes a nice six-figure salary and owns his own home in Austin, Texas, a block away from a great pub with live music every night, but he just can't stop thinking about being a higher earner. Let's find out more about what's going through his mind.

Q: What is the thing you want to manifest?
Alan: I want to make a lot of money.

Q: What does that mean to you? What does the experience look like? (What wounds are you trying to pacify?)

Alan: I can buy a big house and go on fancy vacations, and I'll have the validation of my peers.

Q: Making more money means you have to work more and take on more stress. Do you want to work more and take on more stress? You'll also likely have to compete with people for higher positions. Do you want to do that?
Alan: Yes, I love the thrill of the chase.

Q: Taking on more hours might mean you don't have time to enjoy all the fruits of your labor. No vacations for a while, and no time to enjoy that big house you bought. Is that something you are willing to give up?
Alan: Hmm . . . I hadn't thought about that.

When we stop to consider what our manifestation brings—and what it takes away—we will gain more clarity about whether we actually want the things we think we want.

If we decide we want to keep things as they are, then at least we know that we came to this place based on our own choices. If you decide you want to stay addicted to work, a certain size, to being a scattered person—then own it. Stop shitting on yourself for not changing. Recognize there might not be anything to manifest in this space yet or consider the possibilities that may mean that particular manifestation needs to be refined into something that will be in your better interest.

Growth Is Ongoing

In this chapter about growth, we talk about the Growth Point or even a Pain Point, but I also want to emphasize that growth is not fixed but rather ongoing. I may have kept myself from a relationship for a long time because I had not learned to love myself, but staying in a relationship takes work and also requires growth.

My husband, David, doesn't care about a big house or nice things. He cares about his kids, making sure they eat and anticipating their needs. He enjoys the simplicity of life and wants things to be straightforward.

Me? Well, you know me a little bit by now! I love fancy, romance, extravagance. I love big, complicated plans and epic dreams. I love my ornate home with all its archways and elegance. Meanwhile, big, complicated things cause David anxiety. When our anniversary was coming up, I was so excited about the idea of a trip to New Orleans. The magnolia trees, the champagne cocktails, the mansions in the Garden District . . . it all sounded absolutely dreamy! (Plus, I'd never been.)

Where did David want to go?

St. Louis. It's a three hour-drive away. We've been a bazillion times. He also suggested we drive 45 minutes north to a B and B. I want adventure! He wants ease and simplicity. We have totally different ideas about what a trip should look like. We ended up going to New Orleans with some travel points, and it was all right, but to be honest, it was a little stressful with my toddler and exhausting. I could say I even felt a little let down by this "manifestation." I haven't even looked at all the photos we took.

For my 40th birthday, I want to be in France staying in a gorgeous villa, enjoying good weather, good food, and good scenery. I'm an Epicurean. I live for the senses. I like to celebrate big events. (I wrote this book beforehand so you'll have to check my socials to see if I manifested that or not.) But my husband takes a heavy breath when I mention it, just thinking about how much it's going to cost. Since his birthday is the day after mine, I can't rightfully whisk him into doing something that he's not going to enjoy (but I'm pretty sure he's gonna love it). But say he doesn't. What is it that I'm looking for in this grand vacation? A good time with my husband and kid, honestly. A good time seeing a different place than KC. A time to enjoy good weather, good food, and scenery. Do we have to spend $8k to go on this epic vacation, or would a trip to Carmel-by-the-Sea save us $7k and be extremely enjoyable and memorable as well? This example is not about settling for your dreams but asking yourself why you want what you want and what is truly meaningful to you, what is ultimately going to give you the feeling you seek.

Like that Brianna Wiest quote I mentioned earlier, I might be just trying to create an ideal of the past. When I turned 35, I went to Nice, France, and it was incredible! One day I'd love to go there again, and, you know, one day we might live there. But if I keep returning to past ideals of what I think would make me happy, I won't be open to forging new ideals of what could make me even happier. (Do I really want to take my toddler on another overseas overnight flight after the last one . . . whew . . . maybe not.)

So, here's a Growth Point where I can ask myself: *What am I looking for in France? What does it represent?*

Having a nightcap, walking along the Mediterranean Sea—these all appeal to me tremendously, but I can't say they're my idea of a good life. I have a fantasy of a romantic week at Saint-Jean-Cap-Ferrat, but mostly I want to spend time with David away from home, with a little bit of whimsy thrown in for good measure.

Part of my growth here is to meet my partner in the middle, finding beauty in simplicity and not overcomplicating things. Feeling financially *secure* is one of my Maxims and how I define a good life. (Travel is also a Maxim, but perhaps France will have to wait.) I realized we could do a simple trip and catch up on some bills. That would give me most of what I'm seeking and is in fact more in alignment with all my Maxims. Maybe I'll even go further! What if instead of Mexico next summer, we use the money to finish our kitchen? (I'm turning into an adult!)

Compromises. Shared decisions. The manifestation I called for (a romantic partner) comes with limitations to the life I used to live as a single person. These are some of the changes and growth I am talking about. I have the best husband I could have ever called in, but I lived by myself for a long time. I was used to leaving town whenever I wanted to. It can be a challenge to live with someone else. The manifestation of the romantic partner and family brought me into an awakening and required letting go of some of the freedoms I had as a single woman to go on vacation when I wanted, spend as endlessly as I wanted, and even sleep when I wanted. The manifestation also called me into a space of self-reflection. It always does.

What's more, wherever we go for our vacation, we're going to come home and not feel any different. The joy and contentment—if it's there—has to be there on any ordinary day when we have work to do and a sink full of dishes to clean, not just when we have a Sancerre in our hands and the sun beaming down on us at the beach. If I'm running away from something, then I better figure out what that is because it's going to be right there, staring right back in my face when I get back. I better ask myself what I'm trying to produce in my serotonin levels that I don't have right now. Otherwise, I can go café-hopping in France or as far as star-gazing in central New Zealand, and I'm not going to find the feeling I'm chasing.

We don't necessarily think about the growth required when we formulate our asks, but we will inevitably be pushed into a growth space if we're able to truly receive them.

Are You Bold Enough to Be Happy?

Creating space for self-reflection—this practice is at the center of this book, the core of what I mean by Meaningful Manifestation. As we open ourselves to change, we also open ourselves to the art of redefining what makes us happy. My friend Caleb once said this during a conversation about choosing a partner for his life: "I don't have the audacity to think I know what's best for my life."

I liked the sound of that. Do I have the *audacity* to know? Am I bold enough to know? Because it will require boldness, coming into knowing. It requires an audacity, the change and the growth that's required of us as we level up. His comment was more about how we don't actually know what will make us happy, so we need to remain open. That we often don't evaluate or test what will make us happy and are often running after things of our past makes happiness a kind of trap because we can sabotage ourselves into old patterns of behavior that will keep us from forging a new pathway.

Our tastes are allowed to change, and in fact they should. Building self-awareness takes time. Having the audacity to know what makes you happy means trying out different things. And each time you call something in, you learn more about yourself. After several difficult relationships that affected how he felt about himself, Caleb did the work to find out who he was and who he wanted to be, and I was so happy watching him get married to the love of his life.

Along the way, let's make sure to take the time to enjoy what we have. That kind of presence that we're trying to cultivate might be thought of as an Exhale Point. It's a moment where we take a deep breath and appreciate where we are, how much we've learned, and all we have already brought into fruition. I'll talk more about the Exhale Point in Chapter 9.

Sometimes on this journey, we're going to come up against hard truths. Sometimes what we're tasked with doing is deciding which discomfort we want: the discomfort of trying something new or the discomfort of staying in our comfort zone. Feeling you have to do everything is exhausting and overwhelming, but giving up control and having things go a way you didn't want them to go is difficult as well. Which do you choose?

To me, my baby is the perfect example of how something that's so incredibly meaningful can come with a *huge* amount of discomfort. I always wanted to be a mom but didn't think I would be able to have children. So, I didn't let myself think about it at all. I was fine and accepted that I may never be a mom, but once I found out I was pregnant, I was filled with so much anxiety that I would lose the baby I so deeply and secretly wanted. I then had a baby, and it was like, *Jesus, I haven't slept in two years!* I love my kid more than I love myself, but there are days . . . like right now where she is pulling on my laptop, repeating, "I want a strawberry, please" when I'm up against a deadline and knee-deep in this thought. She's said it 42 times. I had to stop and produce a fruit plate that would keep her occupied long enough to finish this chapter. I wouldn't give it up for the world, but it can be uncomfortable because it's causing me to expand. I'm not a superflexible person. I have focus issues, and it's requiring a level of flexibility I didn't have before. Some days that gets to me. Some days I feel like I'm losing my identity. Some days it means that I can't be selfish or focused on what I want to do or get done. Some days it's meant that my business takes a back seat. Some days it means the house is a mess. Some days it means that I'm overstimulated and so touched-out that I want to be left alone. But this stage of life is so temporary. If I sit around stewing about it all week, I'll miss what is really meaningful about this time in her life where she still needs me. One day she won't ask me for a strawberry; one day she won't ask me to read her "one more" bedtime story. One day she'll be in school, and I'll have my days free to do whatever I wish and will miss being around her 24/7. I miss her when we put her to bed at night. She is my little bestie soulmate, and I could focus on what I don't have, or I can be present with the magic that I'm fortunate enough to experience right now.

I've worked through this process enough now to know where I could choose my reality. If you can get ahead of that sway of energy—whether it's anger, anxiety, or something else—you can completely change the way you see your life. And if you can completely change the way you see your life, you can completely *change* your life.

Which brings me back to storytelling. As humans, we create stories.

Maybe my sister takes too long to text me back. *She must be mad!*

A co-worker gives a big hello one morning. *He must want something from me!*

Are these stories helping or hurting? Do you want to spin your wheels wondering, or would you rather save your energy?

Sometimes the story you have to resist is someone else's version of events. People can bring you into their story, and you get into a fight over which one is true. But you don't need to do that either. You don't have to follow them down that path. You don't need the drama. You can figure things out when everyone cools down a bit.

You get to decide.

In all these cases, what we need is that breath and pause to critically think for ourselves. We need time to ask ourselves these important questions: Do I want to spend my energy thinking this way? Is this the story I want to believe? Do I want to use my energy fighting against this story?

As I wrote at the start of this chapter, I know this is a lot of work, but I'm hoping you are starting to see how much we gain in this process of leveling up and evolving. Whether we bring in something we desire or decide it's not what we want, either way, we're getting to know ourselves better through this process. We're getting to make clearer decisions. *Actually, I don't like spending my evenings that way. Or, I do actually care a lot about this hobby, and I would like to return to it.* We're fine-tuning. We're creating a frame of reference. We're gaining access to the part of us that still needs to be healed.

You can get as detailed and systematic about this process as you like. You can make a chart. Keep a detailed calendar and/or spreadsheet. See where you are putting your energy. How much time does work take up? Where are you devoting time to support your Maxims? What hurdles are you facing? Are they real hurdles? How much is truth, and how much are stories you're telling yourself? Are you unlucky in love because you live in a small town, or would it be just as hard on West 81st Street?

For now, let me end this chapter with this thought: growth is a mindset shift. It comes from having honest conversations with yourself. It is about questioning, peeling back layers, and awakening to a new understanding about yourself. It's about deciding if you want to change or if you want to accept the situation you have now, with the awareness that *you* made the decision to stay with the familiar. Not even in a guilty way but an empowered one. There is a lightness that comes with that awareness. Instead of feeling trapped by your current situation, telling yourself stories about why you are stuck, you own where you are. You decide, perhaps, that the discomfort of change is not, in fact, what you want. That you are okay not writing a novel. That you are okay not taking a big trip. That you are okay staying in your little rental cottage and not trying to buy your own place. You know by now that acquiring was never the goal.

Healing was always our intention.

Chapter 8

Integration

How Do You Apply That Change to Your Life?

Being ready to respond to the creative path which is often illuminated right before us means being present for opportunities as they happen.

— GEORGINA HOOPER

*W*here's the action?

That is the central question of this chapter. We can talk all night—I know I can—but where is the *action*?

In the last chapter, we talked about what needs to change for our manifestation to happen. This is what we are calling the Growth Point. Sometimes, a tremendous amount of growth will take place just by identifying this point. We also talked about some of the things that get in our way—the comfort of familiarity and even the comfort of self-sabotage. Hopefully you have a better grasp now on what it is you are seeking. Change needs to happen to bring us into the life we've imagined. So, let's get to the happening itself.

You might remember from back in Chapter 3, Determine Your Maxims for a Good Life, how a romantic partner was on my top five list. I'm writing this book with my dream romantic partner by my side (or down feeding the kids in the kitchen or out at work, but . . . nearby!), but things looked vastly different just a few years ago.

When I decided I truly wanted to prioritize romantic love, I had to give up seeking out guys who were emotionally unavailable. I discovered that pattern was a bid to prove I was lovable if they loved me back. It was forced and a kind of escape, really. I learned it was a way to avoid dealing with the shadowy aspects of myself. (You can take a guess as to how well that worked out.) The biggest change I had to make was to my mindset. I had to get away from the familiar comfort and self-sabotage of thinking there was no one out there who could love me. *I am the exception! I am so uniquely unlovable.*

This is where I apply my phrase "you're not that special." Some of you might be reading this and saying, "Wait a damn minute." But hear me out. We can tend to form a type of exceptionalism to our circumstances that makes it feel cruelly personal as to why we aren't able to have or be certain things in our lives. We tend to single ourselves out and tell ourselves the story that *everyone else can but not me.* But why not you? What makes you so uniquely terrible that the universe blesses everyone else but not you? What did you do to deserve something so awful as to be left out of the universal plans? Likely nothing. I'm not saying that people don't experience extraordinary hardships and get singled out for their race, sexual orientation, gender, religious beliefs, or financial status. That is a very real reality. But the idea that you or I, 1 in 7 billion people, will not get to experience love makes me say, "You're not that special, Alea." In many ways, you're just like everybody else. You can keep yourself from being vulnerable, continue to be rejected and disappointed, and expect people to treat you badly and somehow protect yourself with the ego boost of what you predicted. (*This is how the universe works. Yep, I knew it.*) That means you don't have to do the work. That means you don't have to open yourself up.

Now, obviously this concept cannot be applied to everything. There are realities in our world that purposefully single out groups through oppression and keep them from manifesting a life they would love. But I'm talking about when we think about the universe and our personal lives, where the government or politics hold no reign, even in some areas where, for example, racism exists. We can't get a bank loan because we're black. That does happen, but there have most definitely been black people who have gotten a loan before, so it is possible. It may be more challenging, but it's still a possibility if you're open to it. Sometimes integration of self is realizing the limitations of our world and becoming defiant in the face of them and not succumbing to their limiting crap.

Or, you can face yourself, realize *you're not that special in this case*, and become truly open to finding an equally capable partner and someone who loves you for you.

Someone who loves me for me. So, what did I decide to do? To start, I got real with my intentions.

Our Intentions put us in a space where we are *in tension* with the thing we're trying to draw forth. I didn't make that up but heard several creators mentioning this concept, and I loved the analogy. It's like an arrow; the moment we decide where we want that arrow, we have to pull back on that string to propel it forward. It's the tension that pushes us somewhere else. It throws us into a space of growth and expansion.

Now sometimes even when we are in the right mindset, there's still a question of timing. I met plenty of emotionally available guys once I shifted the mindset, but it wasn't the time. Maybe these guys still had work they had to do on themselves. I know I always have more work I can do on myself. But it would never be the time until I integrated the change I needed to make in terms of where I was looking for love energetically.

Remember back in Chapter 6 when I told you about my trip to Bali and the epiphany I had during yoga? Well, after that trip, I was at the airport headed to Paris for a Fashion Week job. I had discovered my Anti-Belief—that I had to do everything alone, that I couldn't depend on anyone but myself—and I had figured out what I needed to change. In short, I had to let go of that Anti-Belief. I let go of the idea that everything was up to me.

Did I find the perfect guy over an acai bowl and Jamu juice the next morning? No. In fact, I didn't find anyone in Bali. And I didn't even find someone at the next stop on my journey, the most romantic city in the world.

But things started to change for me vibrationally. In a big way. This can be one of the most energizing points of the IMAGINE process, but you have to be tuned in to noticing the changes in patterns to recognize just how much is actually shifting. Long before we get our manifestation, often we have already healed and changed ourselves in dramatic ways.

I want to highlight this point of the Meaningful Manifestation process, because I think it's a point where some of us might be in danger of losing energy. You've done a lot of hard work to get to this second *I* in IMAGINE. You've figured out your Maxims. You've vetted them and maybe realized some were inauthentic. That itself can be quite a process, letting go of dreams you've had maybe as long as you can remember! You've identified your Anti-Belief or Anti-Beliefs, you've challenged them, rethought the reality you want to live in, and reached your Growth Point. You're now starting to do the hard work of Integration and maybe you look around and you're frustrated to find you still don't have what you're trying to manifest.

I have to bring you back to patience here but also remind you that what we want to see are *signs* that you are changing. What we're hoping for is healing and growth and finding ourselves on a new path. We came into this experience to learn.

The new path is the important part, not where it leads. The path itself is everything.

So let me set the scene for you to give you an idea of what I mean.

I'm at the airport in Bali, wearing a star-studded leather jacket with some leggings. I always get cold on flights. All around me, everyone is in flip-flops while I'm dressed like I'm trekking around Brooklyn in late February. I noticed a handsome brunet guy sitting at my gate who stood out to me because he also had on a leather jacket. *He's cute*, I thought, but then immediately I'm like, *nope*. I take out my *Law of One* book. We all start to get in line to get on the plane, and suddenly he's right behind me.

"I like your jacket," he says.

"I like yours," I tell him.

"That's a very interesting book you are reading," he says.

I am floored because it wasn't a super-popular text.

"I saw your angel wings from across the room." He smiles.

"Bruh, is that a line?" I laugh.

He says it's not a line and tells me I'm an earth angel. (This all happened.)

Bro, this is, like, too much, I think to myself. This was such a stark difference to the way people interact with me in my world.

"I'm not trying to flatter you," he says. "I know people probably flock to you."

"Uh, no. Not exactly. I mean, not that I've noticed." This is weird. He gives me his phone number, walks me to my connection, kisses me on the cheek, and tells me to give him a call. Nothing like this has ever happened to me before. I was never the one being approached by options that seemed actually viable. I take a last look at the island that forever changed me, and I'm in the air.

And I haven't even gotten to Paris yet.

Once I arrived in the City of Lights, I was walking to meet my work friends at the Ritz Bar, and I crossed paths with two handsome black Londoners.

"Hey, where are you headed, luv?" one of them asks me.

"To the Ritz Bar," I responded.

"So are we," one says. His friend looked at him like that was not where they were headed. My friends never showed up, and the Londoners invited me to have a seat with them. We had a long, amazing conversation. He offered to meet me for lunch the next day but ended up oversleeping. I wasn't pressed. I was in Paris, after all. A few days later, he showed up to my friend's fashion show. Out of everywhere in a city of two million people! Not intentionally but because his friend was a designer at the same show. We end up going on a wonderful date, and after four hours, he's like, "I think you should be the mother of my children." Cue the record screech.

What is happening? Never have I had an interaction like this before.

But I knew it was about me. Something was happening. I was changing. My energy was showing up differently. I was starting to heal. I was starting to release the Anti-Belief I'd had since the age of 12 that I had to do everything by myself and there was no one that I could depend on . . . even for love.

What specific actions did I take? Maybe it was the way I carried myself. Maybe it was letting someone hold open a door for me. Maybe wearing a leather jacket on a tropical island and not caring what anyone else thought. Maybe it was saying yes to a glass of champagne on the Place Vendôme when I'd had another plan in mind.

But do you see what I mean about how even though I was far from finding a romantic partner, I was on a new path? Stay with me here. Think about how you might be on a new path. What feels different as you go about your days? Are your interactions with other people changing? Are you able to spend more time away from your phone, more time listening and observing the world around you? Have you gotten any unexpected messages? Have you learned something from a person you'd largely discounted? Found the perfect book you didn't know you were looking for in the basement of a used bookstore?

I'd gone a lifetime feeling invisible, but when I realized I'd been the one closing myself off, keeping myself separate—once I had the eyes to see it and change—I saw the stories I'd told myself hadn't been true. People were drawn to me and attracted to me.

We Actually Didn't Need to Have Paris

Are you ready to activate the physicality of putting a change into practice? This is where you hold yourself accountable. Paris felt so good every time I went. I had often romanticized any time that I had spent there, yet it turns out yet another change I had to integrate on this journey was letting go of the certainty I had that I would find love only in Paris.

Let's go back a few years to when I was living in New York. I tried to get a visa to move to Paris. I was 100 percent sure I was going to get it sorted out. The landlord wanted to know if I was going to extend my lease for another year, but I was hesitant because I hadn't received my visa yet. The person at the visa office said I would for sure get it. On faith that my intuition was right in doing this move, I moved everything out and pared down into three suitcases and lived with a friend while I waited.

I really believed I absolutely *had* to move to Paris to find love. I'd always had an easier time dating there. *There's nobody who loves me here,* I told myself. It was a nine-month process applying for this visa, and I trusted my intuition with everything I had to let go of my lease in New York. But upon going to get my envelope that would change the course of my entire life, I read (in French): *We regret to inform you that your visa has been rejected.*

I didn't get my visa and felt like my world was crumbling around me.

But this was something I was supposed to manifest right? WTF. I did everything the books told me, and now I'm left homeless with nowhere to go except back home to Kansas City with my tail between my legs after I swore I would never move back. I just knew there was no one to meet in Kansas City. I had in fact dated there for years with *zero* luck.

We tell ourselves a lot of stories to avoid being vulnerable. We have to constantly ask: Is it true, or is it a story that we're telling ourselves? Often, we tell ourselves stories to keep ourselves safe. Remember, the ego would rather be safe than happy. My ego feels good telling me that I can find love only in Paris. Then if I'm stuck in New York— or Kansas City, for that matter—and can't find love, well,

See? I was right. Ego likes to be right. Ego doesn't like to be proven wrong.

I stewed that my plans had been foiled, and I felt tricked by the universe. I was calling my guides all kinds of expletives because I felt betrayed deeply that I trusted them and my life got blown up. I was close to losing my whole belief system drowning in the anger of my disappointment. I'll never forget this: I was standing in the kitchen, when I could hear that soft voice of one of my guides: "Why did you want to move to Paris, Alea?"

"Because I wanted to learn the language and pursue my art career there."

"Don't bullshit me, girl. Why did you really want to move there?"

I thought for a few minutes. "Because I think it would be easier to find love there."

"Yes, and if in four years, you didn't have a husband or a family, would you have thought that that manifestation would have been a mistake?"

Damn, that thought hadn't occurred to me. I had such tunnel vision about that possibility that I didn't consider that I could get there and things could not have panned out. And why did she give me such a specific number?

But eventually I was able to let this story go as well, the story that I was only lovable in another language, in another country, eating a chocolate croissant and drinking a café au lait in an outdoor café. This was part of holding myself accountable for my own life.

Finding Love

Fast-forward a couple years, and I arrived back in Kansas City two days before they closed the borders due to COVID.

For two months I stayed inside. Keeping up with the podcast was all I could manage. That and talking to Lexi, my friend who is a spiritual person and let me stay with her for a few months because I had no apartment in KC anymore. Together we were learning and growing, becoming more aware of our blocks, and the things we struggled with. Quarantine with Lexi was another incubation space like Bali where I was opening up, readjusting, realigning, learning how to surrender. All this was part of the process of Integration. I wasn't walking on the Avenue des Champs-Élysées any longer, but I was still on that new path that began to form in those foreign cities.

The main action was exchanging the vision I had of me closed off to the world with the new version of me as someone who could let others in. I may have begun the work of receiving when I accepted the money for the trip to Bali from my new friend. I knew I had to loosen my grip on the outcome of things.

I recognize that quarantine was a traumatic event for a lot of people, but I enjoyed the quiet time. Something big had shifted in my life, and while I no longer felt that I needed to do everything myself, I was quite happy being *by* myself. It's like knowing I wasn't in charge of everything released me into just enjoying my own company.

Eventually I got the money together to get my own place on the plaza, which was a manifestation in itself. It was a penthouse apartment four floors above where I lived before I left. It had a beautiful balcony with tall archways, like my little ivory tower in the sky where I could live peacefully for a little while. But before you all start thinking I'm fancy, this apartment was $1,000 a month, which was a steal compared to everything else that was available. The owners were giving me a deal. But the difference between the last time I was here and now was that I was fully owning being single.

Change was in the air outside my windows as well. The George Floyd protests flooded the streets. I could hear chanting much of the day. There were sirens and protests happening close by, and even though COVID was running rampant, people still showed up to the cause. I was watching this collective trauma, thinking about our uncles, our brothers, and our dads. I was living in a city with a lot of prejudice, a different kind of racism than I'd experienced in New York, which had been more subtle. Here in Kansas City, the racism is black-and-white to the point that a developer literally split the city in half to have a segregation line that kind of still exists today. It's obviously not enforced, but there is a street that basically splits the wealth from those less fortunate. That is changing with gentrification, but it has been bad like that most of my life.

With the time to myself and the ability to be present, on an energetic level, I felt called to check in on black men. I went on Bumble, a dating app, and simply asked, "How are you doing? How's your heart?" to the black men in my city. I didn't get far before I met David. We decided to meet up for coffee. But first I wanted to talk to him on the phone so I could hear his voice. This is as good a time as any to mention that I'm clairaudient—that's often how I make decisions about people, or things. I can gather a huge amount of information from the sound of someone's voice or by listening to my guides.

"I'm not sure what you want me to say, but here is my voice. This is really awkward. I hope this is enough or what you wanted," David said.

It was.

Among the protests, in the midst of the quarantine, we met up at a coffee shop. When we met up, he gave me a hug, and boom! I was transported back to a dream I had that past February 22 (222), which I had written down in great detail. In the dream I was eating pizza with my sister on some monument steps that looked like the Nelson-Atkins (KC's local museum), and a man who was marching with eight black men in protest walked up the steps and asked, "Are you single?"

"What do you want? Why are you bothering me?" I asked.

He took my hands and led me inside to a room that looked like it was from the Regency period. Velvet curtains, mahogany wood, a crystal chandelier, and white candles reflected in ornate mirrors. We danced. I remember noticing his big, rugged hands. When we got to the end of the dance, he asked if I'd like to join him in the back room.

"I know what happens in the back room," I said.

He was suddenly mixing a cocktail for me. "Would you like to have sex?" he asked.

"I knew it!" I said. "I knew you were all about sex."

He sighed, "I wasn't finished. Do you want to just have sex, or do you want your equal and capable partner?"

Duh, the second one.

"Then wait for me."

I was suddenly back to the present moment, looking at this man's hands.

Don't let him know you're crazy yet. Don't tell him your dream. We talked for four hours. Later, back at home when I went to open the app, David's profile was gone. Unbelievable! He ghosted me! I was used to that with online dating, but I centered myself and recited the aspects I had integrated. What's meant for me won't miss me. Clearly I was on a new frequency, and that's what mattered. *Don't go into panic mode*, I told myself. Anyway, I just wanted to support black men, not find someone, so there wasn't any need to panic.

My phone rang. It was him. When I asked him what happened to his profile, he told me he got rid of his profile because he didn't want to see anyone else.

This, I was not used to. Especially after dating in New York. It would take three to five business days for a "hey" and three to six business months for any hint of exclusivity.

It turns out I did not need to go to Paris to find love. It turns out I didn't need to go *looking* for love at all. What I had to do was change the way I thought about myself and love found me. All I had to do was open my heart.

What Action to Take If You've Decided Not to Change

Okay, yes, France, romance, Kansas City, finding true love. All well and good, but what if you've done all the work of considering your Growth Point and your resistance to changing, including digging into your past wounds and facing your pain and fear, but you've decided you do not want to change?

This is a pivotal moment for growth as well. I could have continued to pursue Paris, but the universe was almost forcing me to stay put until I was ready to surrender to give me the very thing I wanted. It just didn't look how I thought it would. Are you finding yourself in a similar spot? Have you wrestled with yourself at a profound and precarious Growth Point and grown enough to decide you're not ready to change? In that case, the action you take might be whatever will facilitate letting go. One of the first things I hope you'll do is, as I wrote in the last chapter, stop shitting on yourself. Acknowledge your un-ready-ness. Being unready is an option as well.

This idea that you stop shitting on yourself means that you have to stop beating yourself up about what you're not doing. You've given it a great deal of thought, and it might not be right for you right now. You're not a bad person because you're not ready to move forward. And it means that you clear that goal out of your way. If you decide you're okay with not learning Russian, perhaps give your language books away to a neighbor or put them in an out-of-the-way place where they won't irritate you. They don't need to be staring you in the face from the nightstand, making you feel bad and taking energy from other pursuits.

If you're not planning to move, you can stop searching houses on Zillow. (Unless you just endlessly enjoy searching houses on Zillow for fun, in which case, go ahead.) If you're not going to train for a 5K right now, stop paying for the running app and use that time intentionally to do something else. It could be you would rather take a walk around the neighborhood or even take a nap. You decide!

Take out your phone, notebook, or journal, and a pen, and reflect on the following questions.

What can you do to energetically let go of the manifestation you're ready to put on hold or give up?

What can you do to clear space for a different goal or greatly needed rest?

What action can you take to commit yourself further to your decision?

The thing is, in our culture at least, we are constantly tasked with the idea of progress. That we should be constantly in motion, constantly improving, and if we aren't, we are lazy, undisciplined, or unmotivated. We are told to consume more, want more, do more without ever considering if that is actually something we want or is even good for us. Some of the happiest people I've met are the people who have the least amount of material things. But some of the biggest struggles are trying to keep up with what society says our life should look like. Why do you want what you want? Make sure that you want something because it's your authentic desire, not because you're trying to keep up with the Joneses . . . or Kardashians.

Manifest a Mindset

We live in a large house. Owning a house like this was a dream I have had for 21 years. In fact, for several years, I used to drive by *this specific house* all the time. I used to live down the street, in a cute but small two-bedroom home, and how I would dream of one day living here! It wasn't too expensive—it's not in the nicest neighborhood—but it fits all our needs.

I love the character, the details, and the archway. They don't make homes like this anymore. I love our vintage décor. I love how we've painted it, the blue wallpaper we put up, and the pictures we've hung. Not gonna lie, it is a constant project. (My husband is overwhelmed by the constant changes and updates, and this is not necessarily the house he would have chosen.) Nevertheless, we've both poured our heart and soul into this home.

And yet, sometimes I want to move.

Now that I've gotten this thing I wanted to manifest forever, I find myself thinking about how much less stressed I would be in a smaller house. We don't need all this space. We certainly don't need these bills. You can't imagine the cost of what it's like to heat this house through radiant heat. If we bought a new house, we would definitely buy a smaller one. This awareness is part of the process of finding out about ourselves, refining our asks, making better choices, and bringing through better manifestations.

If I'm not thinking about moving, I decide the house needs a new project. This is how I work through my anxiety, creating something to focus on instead of the anxiousness I'm feeling. Reorganizing or buying a new piece of furniture. Creating a sensation of progress.

But I wouldn't have known any of this about myself until we manifested this house. I wouldn't have grown into this knowing.

The manifestation process is unending.

That's why we talk about an Inception Point but not an ending point. Because it is about evolving. I can love my house but also acknowledge the burden and weight of having a big house. Both things can be true.

Throughout my own journey learning about what makes Manifestation Meaningful, I've come to understand it is a continual move away from a material focus. That is not to say a house was not a Meaningful Manifestation for me. It absolutely was. (I had a dream about a house that had a ceramic red roof, before we were ever thinking about buying a home.) We have shelter. We have a beautiful place we enjoy spending time in. We have room for the kids, an office for me, a playroom, and a beautiful wraparound porch with concrete planters.

It's not perfect, and we still hear gunshots outside at least monthly, but it has been a dream come true that we not only have a home, but also the means to afford to pay the mortgage every month, pay our utilities, and take care of our children. That's more than I could ask for, yet I'm in the habit of always asking for more.

The focus for me is continually moving away from the idea of a beautiful house and more toward what will take place inside it or what it will facilitate. We are looking deep into our lived experience here on this journey. Imagination, intuition, and other spiritual shit. So much of this is invisible, at least at first. So much takes place in our hearts.

Time with my family is most important. If we have a house that is really big or expensive, that might mean I need to work all the time and cannot see my family. In that case, the house is in conflict with my Maxim about time with family. Maybe I want a cheaper and smaller house where I only need to work part time so I can have more time with my family.

The same can happen with a fancy car. Maybe that's been a long-time dream of yours, but having it requires you to work so much you have almost no time left over to enjoy the car. That's not going to contribute to ease and peace.

I'm not here to demonize people for wanting big houses or fancy cars or dresses that make you feel opulent. My parents loved pretty things. As I've mentioned, we were really poor, but growing up, they surrounded us with things that looked nice. They loved going antiquing. My dad has an insane eye for quality antiques at garage sales and auctions, and people could have easily mistaken us for wealthy if they came to our house because of what my dad could find that was super cheap. I have this amazing wooden lamp that I begged him for when I moved into my own place, and my obsession with Home Goods is definitely his fault. He used to get large boxes of used or costume jewelry for $1 at the auction house, and it fueled my love for jewelry as an adult. It's kind of an obsession; for me it's like wearing art. I'm not telling people they don't need the pretty things. Sometimes you want something because you're human and it's enjoyable! Indulge, my friend, only if that thing is for YOU. Not for anyone else. I feel pretty when I wear lovely gold jewelry and my nontraditional yellow-gemmed wedding rings, and it elevates my energy. I'm just here to remind you to keep asking yourself what it is you really want. *What are you really seeking? What desires are authentic? What's underneath them? What really matters?*

I've written that part of what we're doing here is manifesting a new mindset. I want to help you get into a space where we first recognize the privilege we have to practice manifestation and second recognize the privilege of this learning process we are on. At the same time, we have to keep in mind that progress isn't always good. Sometimes we progress in an unhealthy state from a wound, and we'll realize we don't want to be where we are. We live in a system that prioritizes drive over human life. So, we have to keep resisting that and keep coming back to our life as humans and what we really want to get out of this incredible opportunity we have to be here.

All these things we ask for, receive, and then reflect on reshape and expand us for what is coming next. Who are we becoming next? We are empowering ourselves to make choices and to follow through on them.

It's all nuanced and complex. Such is growth. Such is life.

My clients often ask, "What is my purpose, and how do I make sure I'm pursuing it the right way?" The right way. These questions and this framework feel so heavy with obligation, pressure, space, not doing enough, not being enough, and artificial goals or things we need to do to feel we're progressing in one way or another.

Who said there's a right way? Who said you need to find your purpose and commit to it indefinitely? We don't have to prove our existence on Earth. We don't have to put all kinds of expectations into what we're doing. When we constantly want to be in a different space from where we are, we find ourselves continually suffering.

Can my purpose be what I'm doing right at this moment? Can I feel satisfied by being in a place where I don't have to fear the mess? Where I can just be?

I don't think people do something for themselves enough. Just for themselves. Not for financial security, not for self-improvement, not for someone else.

Ask yourself: *Am I okay with me as I am right now?* Is there anything meaningful you are manifesting from your soul right now that is helping you become the most authentic version of yourself, no matter who is watching? I think once you can get to where you are living the highest expression of yourself, you will think, "I have a good life."

Chapter 9

Noticing

We are now at one of my *favorite* steps in the IMAGINE process—Notice. Oh, how I love noticing! You've done a lot of the messy digging, and now it's time to look up and start seeing what dazzling things are on their way.

Noticing happens at all stages, and I gave some examples in the last chapter—Integration, which is applying the changes that need to be made to move forward—about seeing signs that the pattern is changing and that you're on a new path. In this chapter, I'll go deeper into the intuition aspect of the IMAGINE method. Sharpening our intuition is not a step in the IMAGINE process; rather it is an essential foundation for all of them.

Just to recap:

I is for Inception: Where are you starting?

M is for Manifestation: What do you want?

A is for Anti-Belief: What is the belief challenging what you want?

G is for Growth: What change needs to happen to get what you want?

I is for Integration: How do you apply that change to your life?

N is for Notice: Observing the signs and syncs to help you produce more of it.

E is for Expansion: What do you do once you have realized your manifestation?

So, where do we begin with Notice? Why not start by taking a step outside yourself? Watch the doors open now that you've started to do the work. Look for signs that you are growing. Leaving Bali, I noticed—it would have been hard not to—that men were suddenly interested in me. They were approaching me and saying wild things about angels and, later in Paris, about being the mother of their children. That was a Notice moment. It signaled that I was starting to heal from my childhood wound of taking everything on my own shoulders and keeping others out. Those shoulders that once pulled me up onto the parallel bars and for decades carried the weight of feeling alone were lighter. I wasn't looking for this attention. I was just feeling more centered, moving through the world with more ease.

While I'd rooted out my Anti-Belief, accepted my Growth Point, and integrated change, I'd also surrendered to the process. I was putting myself in the position of receiving, not chasing, not clinging to expectations. When you surrender, you stop trying to control *how* something is going to come into your life. You leave that to the universe. You trust that you've aligned yourself with the right frequency and will start to attract what you desire.

During the trip to Paris after my awakening in Indonesia, I took a step outside myself, looked around, and thought, *I'm doing this. I've opened myself up.*

Things had changed for me energetically. I had changed things for myself energetically. It felt good to be in that new frequency where I knew I could attract positive attention.

What do you notice you are starting to attract into your life? What patterns are you starting to see? What kind of shifts are happening now that you've perhaps been able to work through and remove energetic blocks? To help us sharpen our awareness, let's reflect on questions that will help us tap more deeply into our intuition.

Take out a notebook, journal, pen or pencil, or your phone, and give yourself some time to let your mind wander in response to the following prompts. When you write, don't censor yourself. Let any thoughts come out onto the page no matter how strange they feel or how clumsy the words sound at first. It may be that you're receiving a message. Surrender to it.

When you were a kid, did you ever feel like you had magical powers? When? Where? Do you associate this feeling with any specific places or objects?

Do you have any ancestors you feel are guiding you? Who are they? How do you receive this guidance?

What are your gifts in life? (Interpret this question any way you like.)

Do you tend to remember dreams? Do you ever feel that you are receiving advice or direction through your dreams?

Where do you get a deep sense of knowing? Do you have dreams that mean something? Do you get downloads? Do you have spirit guides?

What helps you hear your own voice better?

To know what you truly want—and to start noticing how you're drawing those things in—you have to learn to connect to spirit and listen to your body. That means getting away from the bombardment of news and images that surround us on our devices and what you're consuming on a day-to-day basis.

One thing I like to do is get into a hot bath with a lot of Epsom salt and try hard not to be on my phone. Water somehow gets my brain in a space where it's ready for intuitive downloads.

Walking is another way I connect. Just taking the time to move my body. I often create a literal shift in my point of view with a walk. Movement leads to inspiration and new ideas about what to bring into the world. Getting out in nature awakens our senses. Any mindfulness practices such as meditation, deep breathing, yoga, journaling, or gardening can help us activate a more aware state. Many people find activities like cooking, knitting, or sketching help slow down our minds and improve our powers of attention.

What practices help you pay more attention to the world around you?

What helps you access a more spiritual level of existence?

Where can you go to hear your voice better?

You Are on the Right Path

For about as long as I can remember, family members have come through to me in my dreams. My grandmother, a.k.a. Grammy, has always been my guide as far as spiritual shit goes. As she was leaving the world, I sat across from her in the hospital. In my mind, I thought the question over and over, "What happens after you die? Will you please come back to visit me and tell me?" But I didn't say it out loud. It didn't seem right to ask Grammy in the middle of dying. I had recently left my whole Christian belief system behind, becoming agnostic, and I didn't want to be on the wrong side of the truth. I was fearful that perhaps if I was wrong, hell in fact was waiting for me. I needed to know that trusting my renunciation of my Christian faith was the right decision. She passed that night.

A week after she passed, I had an incredibly impactful dream. I walked into my grandma's house. She was lying on a small cot, and her body was small, like that of a 10-year-old, but her head still looked like an adult, like her energy was withering away. She was surrounded by two large faceless beings that were ready to take her to the beyond. The floor beneath her started to turn into a circling portal.

I walked in, and she grabbed me quickly. "I don't have much time. Come here." She said first, "It's a girl." At the time, my sister and cousin were both pregnant. Maybe it was one of them? She then gave me some private information about my mom, and she told me to thank her for what she did for my grammy after she died—things I had no idea about. She told me things about other family members, and then a burst of people came through her French doors like they were going through doors on the New York subway. People came rushing in like they had somewhere to be! Right before my eyes, the two entities picked her up and began to take her away. As I watched her start to leave through a portal in the floor, she said, "Oh and about your question, the one you asked me in the hospital? You are on the right path. It's not like how you have been taught (from your parents). I will be your guide. We will take you where you need to go so you understand more."

She started to go through the portal, and in the dream, her clock above the fireplace said 5:55. And when I woke up, it was 5:55 exactly. That moment was an ushering in of a new spiritual journey. It was an opening.

In the months that followed, both my sister and cousin delivered their babies. Both had boys. In the opening of the book, I mentioned my fertility issues. They were severe. I was told for years I was not going to be able to have a baby.

One day a few months into dating David, I thought I was pregnant and the first thing he said was, "I would love to name my child Cairo."

What?

Quick backstory here: I truly believe I had a past life in Cairo. I love Egyptian stuff, and I wear a scarab. I've always wanted to visit this sacred country. And he wants to name his child Cairo? Seriously?

Well, it turns out I wasn't pregnant. I was surprised to find myself disappointed.

David asked me if we should try, and I said to him, "I don't know. I feel like I need a sign." I was on my phone when I said it, and 30 seconds later, I saw this post from Tia Mowry about her vow renewal. It read: "Here is a photo from our 5-year vow renewal, but on our 10th year anniversary, we didn't renew our vows because I was way pregnant with Cairo." I practically threw the phone across the room.

I tell my followers and my friends *trust the signs*. That meant I had to as well, right?

We decided we were going to try, just for a month. I couldn't face the idea of trying for years, putting myself through that physical and emotional upheaval. So just one month. If it was meant to happen, it would. *Universe, what do you have for me?*

I almost died when it happened, but I gave birth.

To a baby girl.

To Cairo Veda.

My grandma told me a decade earlier that I was going to be a mom (insert head exploding emoji here).

Now, I'm not going to assume that all of you have the same kind of weird symbolic or even prophetic dreams I do. Some people tell me they never remember their dreams at all. The sign I got scrolling online and finding Tia Mowry—that was pretty obvious especially after I'd literally just asked for a sign. I'd be willing to bet there are things like this happening in your life as well, if you keep your mind open to them. The signs are all around. Trust them.

What I also know is that when you are on the right path, like my grandmother told me I was, you're going to start experiencing more and more magic. You're going to start seeing repeating sets of numbers that people call *angel numbers*, like the 111s that stalk me. What does it mean?! Just take them as nods from the universe like "Hey, fam, we see you. We are with you." You're going to find symbols that resonate. Exquisite synchronicities. Feathers falling out of the sky or manifestations that you wouldn't have dreamed of just landing in your lap. All kinds of confirmation that the things you're asking for are on the way. You're going to start feeling that the universe is there for you, talks to you, and supports you.

I know you're going to come to love this stage in the process as much as I do. You're going to start feeling how powerful you are when you are clear about your intentions, your decisions, and what matters. You have favor. Daily you will feel newly revived and more alive. You'll start to generate things you haven't even asked for. You're going to get an extra pastry in a French patisserie, find a parking spot on 34th Street during the Macy's Day Parade, run into a friend you'd lost touch with from decades before in a strange town far from where both of you live.

Start by releasing fear, releasing control, opening your hands and eyes, and maybe even inviting the universe to show off for you. I sometimes yell "Universe, show me how good I am. Show me that I'm down here, killing it. Reward me with the fruits of my labor. Go on . . . prove it!" With a grateful mindset, with a true intention to enjoy your experience and notice the signs around you, you will start to see magic everywhere.

Let me take this moment to tell you a few more stories about the magic I've seen. Or maybe I should say the magic I've unleashed.

The Other Girl Was Me

Are you a fan of New Year's Eve? What is your favorite way to usher a new year in? In 2016 I wanted to go absolutely *epic* for New Year's Eve. Let's set the scene because I was already inside a manifestation by swimming in the infinity pool at Marina Bay Sands Hotel in Singapore. It's a pool that looks like a giant boat. I had saved up enough to be able to go on this incredibly special trip on the other side of the world. I got to fly there for basically free in first class because my sister was working at Delta at the time. I was on this high that made me feel like anything was possible. From everything I had learned in *The Secret*, I just wanted to use the frequency of what I was feeling to manifest bigger and better things. It was Thanksgiving, so New Year's Eve was just around the corner. The thought did cross my mind: *Who do you think you are? You just took this big trip across the world, and now you want even more?* But I ignored that voice and said, "The hell with it. Why not?" I started to make a vision board of the New Year's Eve I wanted and looked for opportunities that would present themselves.

On the trip to Singapore, I entered a big hotel with a reservation for the lowest-grade room. For five years, I'd had this beautiful hotel I couldn't afford on my vision board. There I was, standing in the lobby! It was incredible to be standing there, but I was superbold in those days. I knew I was going to manifest a better room. *I have favor*, I told myself. The woman at the counter had a unique haircut. I said that I loved her haircut, which was true. She said she had just gotten it cut and was worried maybe it was too edgy. "No, it really suits you," I said. (It did. I loved it. I wish I had a picture of it I could show you.) I told her it was my first time staying there and how I'd wanted to come there for years.

The woman pulled out my reservation number, saw the room I had booked, and said, "I think I can get you an upgrade." *Ka-ching!* I thanked her and stepped inside the elevator. It went up and up. It was almost a penthouse. I had paid for the ground floor. The views were insane.

Sitting at the top of Marina Bay in Singapore was where the epic New Year's Eve plan started. I was in the energy where I said, *Hey, I've been able to attract something from nothing to come to this.* That gave me the audacity to ask for a wild, unforgettable last night of the year. This was an expansion point for me. I rode the wave of this frequency.

Back home, I asked the universe for an epic experience for December 31. We didn't have the money for this right after a long vacation, but I adjusted my schedule anyway. I found a dogsitter. I bought the dress. (Maybe more than audacious—I was even a bit more *delulu* back then. Maybe that's why it worked better!) I researched NYE parties or dream vacations that I could win but didn't find anything. Yet I was committed to looking for signs. If I hadn't been observant, I might have missed the cue that the epic NYE was on its way.

I held my arms open.

I want this, I kept saying to myself and to my spirit guides. *I don't know how it's going to come, but it is on its way.*

I was doing a practice at that time of daily pinning to my vision board and spending 10 minutes every day when I woke up focused on what I wanted to draw in. If it was supposed to be aligned, I was sure as hell going to bring it into alignment.

Did I really need this trip? Well, no, I didn't, but I think I was excited about the ability I had to change my reality. That felt like a power I never had before. I wanted to test it, research it, see if this was something that I could hone. And as a baby manifester, I think the universe threw me a bone—a big-ass bone.

One of my best friends posted on Instagram about an upcoming Moët competition taking place in NYC, and like clockwork, there it was! The opening I was looking for! They were taking entries to win a trip to NYC for two and to give a toast in Times Square on New Year's Eve in front of millions. An experience of a lifetime.

And it required more action. To enter, you had to post a picture of yourself along with the person you'd like to bring to the NYE party. I went to the Moët site and studied as many photos as I could. Their style. Their branding. *What do they like? What's on brand to them? What feels good to them? I'll do that. Let me use what I notice about them to bring this opportunity into alignment with my life.* This was a period of active Notice—in other words, research.

I had three Instagram accounts. I put different photos in each, all modeled off the Moët branding I'd studied so carefully.

When I was chosen as a finalist, they told me they decided unanimously. Out of 7,000, I was the top three on their list. "It was really between you and this other girl," Paige, the VP of communications told me, and she showed me the account. Turns out the other girl was also me.

In this process, I was able to ask, open myself up to whatever opportunity came, research, and find myself receiving abundantly.

And along the way, there was a trust of intuition. Did I know I would enter a contest for a champagne company? I had no idea. Did I know that scrolling online was going to bring me the sign? Not at all. I just knew that I wanted to do something and wasn't attached to the how, just open to the what and keeping my eyes peeled. When I saw it, it was so painfully clear that I didn't question it at all, just like I wasn't looking for my husband online. The universe brought our paths together. But it was so evident, I didn't question it.

In Times Square, surrounded by paparazzi and screaming people, I was ushered in by security like I was a celebrity. I walked in there, soaking it all in. An amazing experience—truly epic like I'd asked for—but I had already known it was going to happen.

And I knew I would move to New York someday, which I did, eight months later.

I was audacious in my asks. I was outlandish. I held a confidence vibrationally.

So, it's kind of the chicken-before-the-egg kind of thing. Which came first? Did I know that it was going to happen, or did it happen because I put that into motion? Maybe both? But I'll tell you for sure that it wouldn't have happened at all if that wasn't where my attention was and if I wasn't committed to noticing the signs that would follow and tell me where to go.

What told me that was the competition to enter? My intuition. What told me to mimic Moët's branding? My intuition. What informed me on what photos to choose? My intuition. What told me to get a dogsitter ahead of time and get an amazing dress? My intuition. Noticing the signs can sometimes just be the small voice in your head telling you each step of the way.

I've always been tapped into spirit, so I have a plethora of pretty glaring signs. I know that won't always be the case for all of you (it isn't always the case for me) reading this book, but I figure the more stories I share, the more you'll get an idea of the magical possibilities that are out there.

Things can get more subtle as well. And here's something cool: observing the signs and synchronicities will help you produce more of them and your connection to them. Your brain will start to prioritize that information. Start with the obvious, and work your way toward the more hidden. You know how when you first look at the night sky, you might only be able to see a few stars, but then your eyes adjust, and you start to see more and more because you're paying attention? It's kind of like that.

We're now in a state of receiving and recognition. And we could only get here because of all the active work we have done. First, thinking about what makes a good life for us. Then determining our Maxims for a Good Life. Locating our Inception Point. Figuring out what we want to Manifest. Identifying our Anti-Belief. Getting real about our Growth Point. Doing the work of Integration.

All that has brought us to the point where things are starting to shift. And that's what we're noticing. Good things are on their way! They might not be here yet, but they are coming.

As you go about your day, stay present to as many sensory details as possible. A certain bird that lands on a tree branch outside your window. What kind of bird is it? Have you seen it there before? Do you have any specific associations with that bird?

You enter a room in someone's apartment and get a whiff of something nostalgic. Who or what does it remind you of? What memories or images flash in your mind?

While we want to sharpen our senses, we also want to relax our expectations about what we're going to see. We don't want to alter the way that something is trying to come in. That's the Notice. It's not noticing a certain number or hearing a certain song. It's being open to any meaningful number you might see or any meaningful song you might hear. Remember the social media post I saw when I was thinking about having a baby. I didn't say, "Give me a sign that I should name my daughter Cairo." I simply asked for a sign about whether or not I should have a baby. It's a delicate dance. It's being open to noticing something that makes you go, "That seems overly coincidental." Like synchronicity. Something is lining up here.

Do you know that feeling?

Have you had it before?

Will you have it again today?

Growth Isn't Linear

When it comes to your growth process, know that it doesn't have to be linear. It's a process of becoming more self-aware. It will happen in fits and starts. You'll have days when things seem to be falling into place, and days where you're completely overwhelmed and confused, struggling to find the signs that you're on the right path. But what this gives us is the chance to keep finding out where we need to grow, what kinds of actions we need to take.

You know how when you're learning a new skill—say, astrology—it can feel like you practice every day and make zero progress looking at this language that you sure as hell cannot for the life of you decode. And then suddenly one day it makes sense. Manifestation is like that as well. Frustrating days. Showing up. Showing up. Showing up.

Then sudden leaps.

What Can You Do Right Now?

Yet another aspect of Notice is becoming aware of what we need to do in the meantime if our manifestation is a way off. Let's say you have wanted to be a vet your whole life, but you don't have the money for vet school. There is a way. It might not be vet school right now. You might work a job for a few years and make money to go to school part time. Ask yourself: *What steps can I take now to set myself on the path I want to take?*

I've talked a lot about my house in this book. But I know I've mentioned that, even though we live in the house we manifested, we might sell it someday and buy a new house. So, what do I do to get ready for this future, even if we're not putting it on the market today?

1. Take care of the house we have and give it as much love as possible.

2. Notice things that need to be done before it comes time to sell it so we can enjoy it while we live here.

3. Give immense gratitude to our home while we refine our ask.

This is part of the process as well, and it requires the skill of observing and noticing.

With everything you notice, you have a chance to pivot. As long as you don't give up prematurely, and you stay detached from the outcome, you can keep getting closer to what you're trying to draw in. With the process of research or gathering data, you look deeper into what you're trying to bring forth. It's not this version. Okay, what about this? Not that version. A little turn. A tiny shift. You become more ready for what it is you're asking for. You're expanding into the opportunity. You're choosing which way you want to point.

We have to look at our situation and notice what it is and what it is not. When it comes to my relationship with my partner, I have described some of the guys who approached me overseas. I also had a series of suitors who did not work out. I could have said, "Okay, this is not happening."

But instead I said, *I'm getting closer.* Things are changing. Things are happening in a new way. That's what we're looking for! You know when you're playing a game looking for an Easter egg or some other treasure, and the person who knows where it is says you're getting warmer or colder? Well, this is when you're getting warmer. You haven't found it, but you're getting so close! Are you seeing a change in patterns? Are you feeling closer to something you've wanted for a long time, even if it's still out of reach?

The foundation of Notice is intuition, and the foundation of intuition is trusting ourselves. We have to trust ourselves to be capable of noticing and, once we do, to not cling so tightly to our old reality that we sabotage ourselves or try to make meaning out of something that isn't there. Sometimes we are so desperate for a sign that we will take literally anything to justify what we are trying to draw in. Noticing means being open but not being emotionally attached to the outcome. Then we can take those little signs in stride without trying to make them mean something they don't. *This* is the hardest part, I have to admit, to do. What's a sign and what's not. You will know if you are in the stage of "Universe, I'm open to what is in my best and highest good."

Storytime. There was a boy who I liked when I lived in New York. We will call him Julien. We had a two-year-long friendship that definitely had blurred lines at times. For Thanksgiving, he came down to visit me after I moved out of New York. To me this was a big gesture, to come down, spend money, and meet my family. I didn't want to make too much out of it, but I was really excited, thinking that this must mean something, right? Thanksgiving comes, and we go down to our town's plaza lighting ceremony (it's a big tradition, people go every year, there are fireworks and such). Anyway, we were down there, having a great time, and we took a selfie together. Well, this selfie was no ordinary selfie, because behind us in the photo was a pink heart in the sky between our heads. Three fireworks had shot into the sky, and at the moment he took the photo, it formed a heart. I have to emphasize that this wasn't a heart-shaped explosive that was meant to do that. No. This was just three going up at the same time and when the exposure clicked, the light receptors captured a heart where there was none. You'd have to see it to believe it. We both thought that was weird, but I couldn't contain myself. I was sure it was a sign. At the end of the night, unprompted, he leans over to kiss me. I'm thinking "Holy crap, it's happening!" But this still, small voice in my head said, *No, stop*. I didn't want to listen to the voice, but I noticed it wasn't going away.

STOP.

So I pulled away. I proceeded to tell Julien that I liked him, and his face turned white. I found out that he didn't *see me that way*.

WTF are you doing here, dude? What is this?

You see, the sign wasn't the heart in the sky but the voice in my mind telling me to STOP. He was the lesson that prompted me to write my second book but not the man I would walk down the aisle with, even though I spent many days fantasizing about it.

But thank God, right? Whew. Hindsight is 20/20, but I knew on some level what was happening, I just didn't want to see it. In that experience, I could have closed up shop right then and there. So many mixed messages and me feeling like an option but not a choice. I still wasn't in a space where I knew what was meaningful to me, which was that I was treated with love and respect and not chasing hearts that were not open to me.

If you have taken all the action you can take and it's still not happening for you, try not doing anything and waiting. Similarly, if you're noticing a lot of stress and resistance, take a step back.

If nothing else, you'll get more clarity on what you want. I know I'm not manifesting anything when I'm forcing or falling in the trap of asking from scarcity mode. (What I mean by a scarcity mode is a frantic kind of feel. Like you have to scramble to make things work—I have to do this and this and this! Like desperation, because trust me, I've been there.)

Are you with me? I tried to implement these ideas in something I called the Good Life Workshop once, and it didn't take off. People didn't seem interested in a good life. They wanted to make a million dollars. But I am not here to teach you to quick fix your life. Maybe someone else can. But pretty soon, I think you'll discover that nothing's going to quick-fix your life. I had to take the steps to notice what I could do in the meantime while I waited for people to be ready to create a good life and appreciate the life they had.

And here we are.

In this process, there is a commitment and a detachment. A desire and a letting go. It's nuanced, complex, and intuitive. Meaningful Manifestation doesn't take place on the surface. We can't be attached to outcomes. We are looking for an opening, not scrambling for outcomes.

We have to mean it when we ask, *Universe, what do you have for me?*

It's like a sensory exercise. What do you see? What do you hear? What do you smell? Your eyes have to be open. That in itself is an action, but it has an ease to it. Receiving. You're not drawing conclusions or making assumptions. You're just observing in the physical realm and the spiritual realm as well. And then you're taking action based on your observations. The more you notice, the more things keep showing up.

With the New Year's Eve plan, it was like my intuition—I was so convinced this experience would come—almost drove my desire. When the opening did come, it was so easy to notice because I wasn't attached to a specific outcome. I had no fear; I didn't book a second option just in case. I knew what was on its way.

A Note about Noticing

I'm a person who likes *big* gestures. I'm like, *It's your birthday. Here's an $800 watch!* My husband, David, is a person who likes everyday gestures. For him, it's those little, everyday kinds of things. And little by little, I'm not talking about cards or flowers for our anniversary. That's not so much him. It used to make me think he's not doing as much as me. I want to be taken care of! I want to be on the receiving end of the BIG gesture that shows how much he cares.

But here's what I mean about the little everyday things. A few weeks prior, I had bought brand-name Honey Nut Cheerios. I was kind of muttering to myself about how Trader Joe's has a much better version of the cereal. And one day I found myself getting the Trader Joe's O's out of the cabinet. Did he remember what I said and go buy this? He did! He remembers little things like the cereal I like. Just tucked in the cabinet without any fanfare, just anticipated my need, because he listens and cares. How sweet is that?

So, when I feel like he's not taking care of me, that's often me just not paying attention. I sat him down, I grabbed his face, and I said, "You love me!"

"Yes, of course," he said.

"No, you really love me." I smiled. I've been trippin'. My expectations were not serving me. They were in fact getting in the way of me seeing how beautiful things are when I'm present to them and open to Notice.

When we talk about Notice, we also want to talk about seeing what is already present. Are you causing yourself suffering by holding on to expectations that are not serving you? Do you have expectations that are blocking you from seeing what is right in front of you?

This is yet another facet to surrender. Surrendering our expectations about what someone would do if they felt a certain way and recognizing everyone has their own ways. To Manifest Meaningfully, we have to be open to the universe we have, not the one we imagine.

Gratitude: Stop and Pause (Exhale)

I want to close this chapter by turning to gratitude. Gratitude is such a major aspect of Notice. The more you think about what you're grateful for, the more you'll be able to draw those same things into your life. To dive into gratitude, I want to describe the Exhale Point. You remember this book promised to help you not only manifest the life you want but also appreciate the life you already have. It's hard to do that if you're always chasing something. It's really hard to do that if you're always looking ahead, always thinking about what's next. As I wrote in Chapter 2, it's "What matters?" not just "What's next?"

The Exhale Point is when we sit on our couch and take a breath. No phone. No TV. No music. Just us taking in where we are in our lives.

The Exhale is not about racing through.

The Exhale is not about bingeing.

The Exhale is not asking someone who got married when kids are coming. Not asking someone who had one child when the second one is coming.

The Exhale is not asking about what somebody's toddler is doing: Are they walking yet? What are you thinking for preschool?

Can we just breathe? Can we enjoy what we have? What is the point in manifesting if you don't get to enjoy it?

The Exhale is giving ourselves time to digest information.

The Exhale is thinking about all the things big and small we've already accomplished.

The Exhale is focusing on what's already here, what's already present, not what is lacking; what is missing; or what is wrong or can be improved, maximized, tweaked, redone, redesigned, or upscaled.

The Exhale is giving ourselves rest points.

The Exhale is peace.

I think the Exhale is pivotal to what I mean by Meaningful Manifestation.

What does an exhale look like for you? What can you do right now, in this moment, to exhale and be where you are?

Ask yourself the following questions:

What am I grateful for now?
What have I grown out of?

What are my trigger points?
What do I expect to happen?
How do I move through the world?
How do I see my own reality?

At this point in time, my job is not doing what I want it to do. I've talked a bit about how I want to move away from intensive mediumship readings. I also want to spend time with my daughter while she is young. I need to change things about the structure of my work. Plus, as I said, there's always something in my house I want to change.

But I have to take the time to breathe and exhale in the middle of this. I have to find points in the day when I say, "This is good enough for right now. I have 1,000 projects I need to do, but I'm in this beautiful living room. I've reinvented my life and reevolved and reimagined this stage, and I get to experience it. I'm so thankful for this."

It's not necessarily about keeping a gratitude journal—although you can if you want to. It's about perspective. It's cultivating a point of view. I'll say it again, changing your perspective will change your life. This is what I meant.

I'm very good at doing. I'm drawn to creating new tasks to do. So, it is work for me to get to the Exhale Point where I can stop and take it in. It's work to convince myself that not everything has to be done at this instant.

I want us to find an easier flow to life. I want us to get away from the pressures of what we're supposed to do and achieve and have. I want us to remove ourselves from the chase. We have to get away from the outward mindset of go, go, go. No wonder everyone is suffering, feeling unworthy.

As Tricia Hersey writes in *Rest Is Resistance*, "Along with stealing your imagination and time, grind culture has stolen the ability for pleasure, hobbies, leisure, and experimentation. We are caught up in a never-ending cycle of going and doing." One day, I hope we can all deprogram from the lie that rest, silence, and pausing are a luxury and a privilege. They are not! The systems manipulated you to believe it is true. The systems have been lying and guiding us all blindly to urgent and unsustainable fantasies. We have replaced our inherent self-esteem with toxic productivity.

Capitalism is a religion. We work until our bodies are in pain. Always a new project. Always a new goal. Never-ending "progress." What are you working on? What's next for you? Why not? How are you doing?

Rather, we should be asking this: How is your heart?

This cultural shift has to happen, a Growth Point on a societal level. Acknowledging this time for rest gives us that moment to exhale. Rest in what you've manifested so far. More is coming anyway, I promise.

In this rest, we're cultivating distance from what we think we want. If we don't get it, yeah, it's disappointing. But it's not life-ending. If this book bombs, it will be hard. But it will still be growth.

Rest is an essential part of growth. A flower does not grow year-round. There is a rest in winter, followed by a rebirth. We don't need to always be doing, always be calling in, always be growing. We can breathe. We can grow underneath in our root systems. We can connect more to ourselves. We have to receive the moment to luxuriate in it.

Isn't it good enough where you are right now?

Look around. *What do you love about the life you're living?* And what a breath of fresh air that can be.

Chapter 10

Expansion

Manifestation is bringing thought into fruition. From a soul perspective, it's playing—let's try all the things. Let's try them over and over again.

During the process of writing this book, I struggled with settling on a title. I thought of 30 alternate titles to the one I originally pitched to the publisher. My editors came up with great ideas. The subject was always going to be manifestation, but the trouble I had with that word was from a diversity lens. A lot of black and brown communities have seen manifestation as a "white" word and space. Many people I speak to associate the word with privilege. For that reason, they feel a disconnect.

What are your thoughts about the word *manifestation*? What are your associations with it? What do you feel about the way I've presented it, as more about healing and self-discovery rather than acquisition? Perhaps we can keep expanding our understanding and interpretation of the word as we undergo our own personal expansions.

I love the idea of manifestation as a practice that can free us from our desires. It feels counterintuitive, and there is a beautiful energy in that. I first heard of this concept from Dr. Brent Satterfield. He introduced this idea to me on my podcast one day, and it punched me in the face.

I will never be the same! I thought. Manifestation as freeing us from our desires.

I wanted to take this idea and run with it. (I have a tendency to take things and run with them, if you haven't noticed yet.) How can I expand on that? Incorporate it in my practice? What does it mean to be free of our desires? Other people have offered the idea that the word *intention* can be reconfigured as *in tension*. Think of a rubber band being pulled and stretched; eventually it can propel us to a new place. When we're in desire, full of intention, in tension with ourselves, we are stretching and trying to level up. This is our Expansion. When we get to that next level, we have in some way freed ourselves from the desire that got us there. We are now free to discover more about who we are.

And now I'm going to grab on to the momentum of this idea and go even bigger. Ready?

If we are all one—a collection of beings that is truly a single being—then our goal must be to figure out who we are as a collective being. The universe is discovering what it is and how it defines itself, and as it does, each one of us is undergoing that same process. We are on separate journeys—I might be obsessed with starting a fine-jewelry design business, and you might be learning to balance on a high wire—but in some fundamental way, you are me and I am you. No matter how different our desires, they all show how aligned we are because we are all trying to set ourselves on the path of discovery and more knowing. Aren't we?

Think of a super-wealthy person who has everything—the mansion worth $35 million overlooking the ocean with an infinity pool, a banquet hall, and 15 bathrooms. Throw in a personal vineyard and private hiking trails. A Ferrari and a vacation home on a clifftop somewhere with views of a waterfall. A collection of trophies and awards. Millions of followers on social media.

Then what?

Now what?

Well, eventually, once they have everything—oh yes, I should have added a private jet—they're going to have to sit with themselves and figure out who they are. At some point, they'll likely realize it was never about the accumulation of things. It was always about learning the depth of their authenticity. Money doesn't make you rich; it just amplifies more of who you are. So, it's not a question of why lots of money doesn't make many of us happy. Instead, it likely feeds a wounded inner child version of ourselves until we are ready to mature. If a big house or fancy car or gorgeous dress are meaningful to you, those can be legitimate manifestations. But eventually you have to do the work to find out where these desires are coming from, bring forth the shadows, and deal with them, no matter what. This alignment work is deep intentional work. It is not lighting a candle, saying a mantra, and hoping for the best.

As I've mentioned throughout this book, those with very little may not have the luxury of engaging in this journey. If you're trying to keep your house out of foreclosure and need to pay for groceries, manifestation at this point in the traditional sense feels like extravagance, an indulgence even. But what if the manifestation is about coming into realization of who you are? That your circumstances are bringing you into an awareness about what you need versus what you want?

You and I have an incredible opportunity to go on this journey of learning more about ourselves. Look around and see what's possible. Look how connected we are to the universe. If people are further ahead than you, that just means they're showing you what's out there and what's available as you figure out who you are and IMAGINE your way into the next version of you.

My whole life, I've been trying to figure out who I am. My mom used to say I'm like Madonna because of how often I like to reinvent myself. I really enjoy the process of deepening my relationship with myself. I'm guessing that if you're reading this book, you enjoy deepening your relationship with yourself as well.

Let's celebrate this opportunity. Let's relish it! Thank your spirit guides or God or the universe for having a chance to manifest meaningfully (not just materially). What good fortune to have the chance to become more rooted and grounded in who you are. To be able to say as new things come in, "Wait, did I want this? Or do I want this slightly different version? Or was I actually more in alignment before I made this change?" Each time we pivot means we are shifting to a higher plane of understanding. It doesn't negate our previous efforts but means we took the lessons and integrated them into our journeys of Expansion. Expansion has always been at the root of our leveling up.

What can we do in our lives to support others in this journey? Well, first, we have to remember nobody is going to change until they're ready.

I'm a natural cheerleader. I have the gift of encouragement. I get excited about others' ideas and try to help them bring them into light.

What do you want to do?
How can I help?
Let's make your dream a reality.
I have a million ideas!

But I've learned that I waste a lot of energy cheerleading people into something they're not ready to do yet. That's energy I can put into doing my own IMAGINING, listening to my own intuition, and deepening my own practices of manifestation.

I think it comes down to asking the right questions. The moment we apply pressure or pass along a message of shame or guilt—You should have done X, Y, and Z by now—we are hurting people's chances of moving forward. It will make them contract. It's a parallel to shaming ourselves for not meeting our own goals, whether those are about healthy eating, improving our tennis skills, or saving money. It will have the opposite effect. We'll contract back into ourselves. We'll recede. Eat an entire bag of chips and skip the gym. Scroll for hours online, even though it makes us feel bad about ourselves. Go out and blow our bonus instead of putting any of it into savings.

Support has to be gentle with others and with ourselves as well.

I've IMAGINED. I've walked deep in my intuition. I've downloaded. I've talked to spirit guides. I've manifested again and again. I've had insane experiences. You've read about many of them in this book. My grandmother foretold my baby girl. I dreamed about my husband. Flying high while in a skyscraper in Singapore, I knew I was going to have the world's most unbelievable New Year's Eve. And I did.

But it's not all perfect. Far from it.

Do I have my ideal health? No.

Do I have my ideal family? Yes. Do they drive me nuts sometimes? I'll leave that one to your imagination.

Do I have financial security? Working on it.

Do I live in Paris? Heck no. I'm back in Kansas City, where I swore I'd never be.

For my 40th birthday, I'd love to go to France. And just by stating my intention, I kick off the IMAGINE process once again.

Q: Why? What does it mean to me to go to Paris?

It would be beautiful and exciting, a core memory that our family would always treasure.

Q: What is my Anti-Belief?
We don't have enough money.

Q: How could I get enough money?
I could work like crazy to make it happen.

Q: Do you want to work nonstop for eight months to spend time in France?
Probably not. I don't think I want to trade all that time with my family during the year so that we can have that vacation that probably won't be as incredible as I'm imagining. The jet lag, the kids' dairy and gluten allergies.

Q: What do I want to feel?
I want an incredible memory with my family.

Q: Do you need to go to France for that to happen?
No, that can happen anywhere.
And that leads me back to surrender. Universe, take care of it. Figure it out. To the best of my ability, I will be open and vulnerable to whatever happens. I will open my eyes and notice. I will stay present.

Q: Does it have to happen now?
Maybe the trip can happen when the kids are older. Would that be any less impactful? Or just my impatience saying it has to happen now? It could be amazing but happen at another time. That would be okay, right? (Check in with me next year.)

I still vacillate between being right in the frequency and having times when I am burned out and don't know if we can make a trip to Arizona, let alone Paris. There are times when I have favor—when I just expect the universe to roll out the red carpet for me—and there are times when paying all our bills seems like a tall order.

I'm letting you know this because I expect you'll experience the same ups and downs when it comes to vibrational energy. This book offers a road map for you and the IMAGINE method, which I believe is one of the fastest and most reliable ways to bring into your life the things that you desire and more importantly the feelings you're seeking, but it's also the story of a real life, and that means it contains the bumps and confusions and the detours that are part of anybody's real life. I share those with you so that you know what to expect and know not to give up, even if you fall out of alignment or if things are not manifesting the way that you hoped they would. Some of it, as I've said, is about patience. Some of it is about flexibility, but a lot is about growing through discomfort and disappointment.

I think one of the reasons people have been drawn to my story besides the miracle of how I was able to manifest so much in such a short time is that I'm pretty straightforward about the obstacles in my path. Even the year that I can point to as definitive proof that manifestation works was simply a portal for me into a new layer of understanding, a whole new process of leveling up.

What guidance can I give you for when things don't work out the way you intended? What if after months of deep, intentional work, you're not where you want to be? That's okay too. Being gentle is part of the work. Say the following words to yourself.

This is not my only chance.
I'm living in abundance.
I'm not living in scarcity.
We are all crafting our own stories.

Remember what my grandmother told me in a dream. "You're on the right path. I will be your guide. We will take you where you need to go."

I hope this book can help you find the right path and serve as a guide, for at least a little while. I'm so excited for the opportunities you have still ahead—the opportunity to manifest the life you want but also keep coming into new levels of appreciation for the life you already have waiting for you when you set down this book. And most of all I'm excited that you have the opportunity to discover more about who you are.

We've all been imprinted with fears and insecurities, many from childhood. Influencers surround us daily telling us how to elevate and optimize and maximize. How to set up a healthy morning routine, make our bedroom a cozy sanctuary, improve our relationships, and make more money. At the same time, we are bombarded daily with messages saying we can't. We can't have this dream job. We can't take time out of our workday for joy. We can't spend more time with family. We're absorbing lessons in pragmatism and accepting limitations. This is how the world works. But what if the resistance holding us back is actually coming from inside us? What if it's our beliefs holding us back? What if we're fighting ourselves? What if we can decide to make a change and that will shift things on some powerful but invisible energetic level?

Last year, I was making so much money, I never thought I'd be in a place where we would have to struggle again. I had found a vibrational match with my podcast. But it turned out I couldn't sustain producing that level of content in the way that I was going about it. It wasn't healthy for me. Longer medium readings, I've discovered, also lead to severe burnout. As I wrote about earlier, I was spending a lot of time connecting with loved ones who had passed in tragic ways, and it was draining me emotionally. So, I shifted to the idea of shorter, rapid-fire readings instead. I also put more energy toward card divination, where the experience is more uplifting. It feels good to be present for strangers, to validate their feelings and experiences and help them center in on what's blocking them from greater awareness.

But I didn't fill everything back up. I left space open. I knew I needed to create a new wave, a new frequency. I knew I needed to find a new vibrational match. The podcast and mediumship had taken up all my time, and I knew whatever next frequency I was going to ride, it couldn't arrive without space for it to materialize. We need to hold space for ourselves to understand what it is we really value.

So I found myself, once more, in a liminal state. In-between and uncertain. I told myself I was not going to hold on to resistance, that something new would find its way to me. I let go. I got out of my own way.

I said, "Universe, what will you have for me?"

You know the story by now. A name I didn't recognize in my DMs. An editor from Hay House in the U.K. "We really like your account," she wrote. "We've listened to your podcast. We like your message."

So, this book project landed in my lap, kind of. But then the hard work began. I tried four book proposals. The publisher shot them all down. They wanted more stories to accompany my methods. By now it's clear I've got plenty of stories. And I'm reaching the end of telling them, for now. What will happen to this book once it goes out into the world? From my writing desk in Kansas City, Missouri, I can only IMAGINE.

But I do know that this book came about because a few years ago, I was frustrated with how I felt after I'd manifested so much and resolved to pursue magic. Magic for me is the feeling of wonder and awe that can be elicited by experiences that seem mystical or extraordinary. This could include the beauty of nature, the power of music or art, or the joy of human connection.

Magic is not just a fantasy but a real and tangible force that you can access in your everyday life just by adjusting your perspective. Pursuing this kind of wonder and magic has made me a much happier person. Isn't it an amazing feeling to be alive? It's so much fun.

It doesn't mean that I no longer wish to improve my life or manifest different experiences, but it does mean I get a higher level of enjoyment out of being able to enjoy the life that I already have. There's also a high level of enjoyment in knowing that manifestation is about teaching us and pointing us toward ourselves. And that shift has brought me a lot more calm and a much greater sense of contentment.

One of my favorite philosophers, Alan Watts, says, "The meaning of life is just to be alive. It is so plain and so obvious and so simple. And yet, everybody rushes around in a great panic as if it were necessary to achieve something beyond themselves." When we internalize this idea, it takes the pressure off us to feel as if we have some grand display to put on besides simply living well by our own standards— by our own philosophy of what makes a good life. Yes, we can manifest bigger and better things, but we don't have to feel trapped by our own desires. We can free ourselves from them. It's a miracle we are even here.

You being here on this earth, experiencing conscious-ness, is nothing short of a divine miracle. Think about it. Earth's distance from the sun is so perfectly calculated that if we were any closer or farther away, the conditions for life as we know it would not exist. The temperature would either be too hot or too cold to support life. And the probability of someone being born with their exact genetic makeup, at the exact moment in time that they were born, is almost unfathomable. And yet, here we are, alive and experiencing the world around us. It's a testament to the power of life and a reminder of how precious and unique we are. Unique and yet alike. Unique and yet aligned.

Is this not a real miracle? That we manage to walk around on this ball of water that is hurtling through space at thousands of miles per hour is just mind blowing. Magic is all around us, waiting to be discovered. It's the kiss of a lover, the twinkle of the stars, and the electricity that keeps our heart beating. It's in the moments that take our breath away and the everyday experiences that we often take for granted. But often, in the pursuit of our dreams and desires, we forget about the magic that already exists in our lives. We get so caught up in the chase for more that we forget to appreciate what we have right now. That's where the pursuit of magic comes in. It's about finding the balance between loving the life you have while still manifesting the life you want. It's about embracing the power of your thoughts and beliefs and using them to create the reality you desire.

If I were to leave the earth today, I would be pissed because my daughter is young. But I also know that with my grandmother as my guide, I have lived a very full life. In my nearly 40 years so far, I've tried to muscle every single drop out of this life that I could. Hopefully that will con-tinue for another 40 or 50 years, but who can say?

Are you muscling every single drop of life you can? Looking for magic wherever you can find it? Maybe there is a better way to live according to your own rules. This is Meaningful Manifestation. Imagining and creating the life you want to live. The path forward is asking questions.

Eventually, you may find yourself in a place where people begin to question you. This is natural, because many of us are caught up in the system that emphasizes money; chasing; constant goal setting; and running, running, running. They may be critical of your decisions. You could be making more money! You could be getting your photographs on the cover of a magazine! You could be traveling the world.

If you're still not happy, it's because happiness is not an effect of what we manifest. True happiness is an inside job. We shouldn't be manifesting to make ourselves happy; we should be manifesting because it makes our lives meaningful and worth living.

Even this thought process is expanding you and what it means for you to live a good life. To listen to your most authentic self and what you need for a better life through your own eyes. Living on your own terms but not missing out on what this life offers in its magic each and every day . . . if we notice it. We might not expect it; we might not have even asked for it. It might even be better than what we imagined if we can wait for it, but we can see, right now in this very moment, the beauty in the process . . .

For this is manifesting . . . meaningfully.

I've had years where I made a lot of money (and worked my ass off) and was traveling constantly. I had years where people maybe envied what I had. And I think a lot of the time, I looked happy on the outside. Now I'm in a place with my family where we are barely middle class. But my highest Maxim for a Good Life is time with my kid. And that's what I have. Maybe when she starts school, I'll pursue a different set of goals. Maybe at some point, we'll need to look for a babysitter or daycare situation. But for today, running after the next thing feels like not appreciating what I have right here.

The minute I step away from this computer, I will find her in the kitchen, asking for strawberries. Or in a room coloring with orange crayon on the walls we just painted. Sometimes she runs into my office just to give me a hug and then runs out again with a "Wuv yew!"

What is your highest Maxim for a Good Life? Is it something always out of reach, or is it something that's waiting for you the minute you open your eyes to see it? Is there something more you could ask for, or could you instead bring yourself into the present moment, whatever it holds?

I'm reaching the end of this book, but I have so much more I want to explore. The *Spiritual Shit* podcast is back up! And though I've scaled back, I'm still doing my mediumship work. That means that each day, a client comes and tells me about the worst day of their life. A mom who lost her son when he was 26. A girl who lost her mother as a young child, whose life is marked by the wound of not having her mom as she was growing up. I'm an empath. Emotional grieving is hard for me. I have a sensitivity that means I can't find any distance from these stories. I cry and cry, sobbing in my bed, as if these things happened to me. And I know we're all one, so it is like they have happened to me. Pain through the generations. But most of what comes through these stories—and the connections we're able to make with family members who have passed—is that the greatest gift the world has to offer is love.

If we're prioritizing all kinds of other things, we might be missing out on this gift. But it's not too late. We're always expanding, remember? You're on the right path. This ever-expanded version of you can take you where you need to go. We're all evolving through these lifetimes, passing on what we've learned through the generations.

Let's go back to that first time I described being awake at 3 A.M. when I looked around and thought, *I have everything I want. Why am I not happy?* What I've learned since then is that we are not asking for things to be happy; we're asking so we can evolve.

It is my wish now to be home with my daughter. This is the life I wanted to manifest. (I've basically switched roles with David, where he is working full time and I'm working part time and at home with the kids.) That might mean less financial security. That might mean being further from my health and travel and creative goals. At the same time, I know it is an incredible privilege to spend these hours with her. But there's no clocking out. There is always more cleaning to do, more clothes to wash or fold. Another snack to prepare and clean up. Another messy activity to potentially stain the carpet. In some ways, I'm more stressed out now than I ever was. It's almost double the work. It's not easy and giddy and smiling every day. But it's what matters to me. It's me in the evolving process. Getting to spend this time with my daughter when she's little is not an easy life, but it feels like a *good* life. There's a vast difference for me, however, between the tired of chasing magazine covers in Milan and the tired of chasing my toddler. I know why I'm doing this. This is important to me. This is meaningful to me.

When people talk about happiness, what they often mean is to be free of discomfort. Am I free of discomfort taking care of my daughter? Hell no. My body hurts. It has been through the extreme trauma that is birth. When I can't sleep enough, like now, my illness flares up. I'm in a lot of discomfort now. I'm often scared and uncertain. And then there are moments when she turns to me and goes "Mommy," and my heart explodes.

Meaningful Manifestation is also, at base, a love story. I think my medium work has shown me that our whole experience here is to teach us about love. How to love others, how to love ourselves, and how to know, when it's our time to leave, that we put our meaningful relationships and experiences with those people at the center of our lives.

Last summer, we took our daughter to the pool for the first time. When I was growing up, my mom was scared to swim—we never went. Standing in the shallow end, my husband wouldn't let her go. "I can't!" he said. "She's gonna drown," he said, only half joking. But my daughter did not want to be confined. Her legs were flailing out. She was bursting to immerse herself into the water, to get into the experience of this life and make it her own. To begin muscling every drop of whatever life has to offer out of the one she's been given.

David passed her to me. I was more scared than she was, but I knew it was important for me not to give in to my fear. I would safeguard her in the ways that were necessary, but I sure as hell would not keep her from trying. So, I gave her a little bit of space, letting go for just a second.

"I'm here," I tell her. "I'm here."

She already knows she can do it.

This child, no longer my tiny baby, starts to swim.

The ending of one thing is also the beginning of another.
What is the next adventure? There is room enough in this
life—with its many endings, its many beginnings—
for things you could not have imagined last week
or last year or [even] ten years ago.

— Maggie Smith

ACKNOWLEDGMENTS

I'd like to mention Amy Kiberd, who gave me this opportunity; Wendy Sherman, my agent; my editors and copywriters; my writer, Rachel Federman.

My husband, David Jones, for his help and support.

My friend, Meg Bartlett, who helped me flesh out my ideas.

ABOUT THE AUTHOR

ALEA LOVELY is a spiritual advisor and metaphysical philosopher who has practiced as an intuitive and energy coach for the last seven years. She is the creator and host of the podcast *Spiritual Shit*, which has topped the charts, gaining a #1 spot on iTunes in America.

Growing up super religious, Alea found that a large part of her life didn't align with her own identity because, as a child, she was having a host of spiritual experiences she couldn't explain that made her feel ashamed of her spiritual sensitivities. Seeing ghosts, hearing ancestors, prophetic dreams, and empathic experiences fell on deaf ears, were met with weird looks, or were criticized. She felt she had to hide the biggest part of herself for most of her life, until a major move forced her to awaken back to herself and reclaim her purpose. Alea knew it was time for her to claim her whole self again; and since then she's helped thousands of people awaken back to their true selves through energy coaching, card readings, public speaking, and her podcast.

Alea opened the door to meaningful manifestation and learned how to see the world through a lens that allowed her to experience more magic in her everyday life. It is her mission to help people understand how to do the same and find deep fulfillment in their lives by creating a deeply magical one to live.

Website: **thelovelyalea.com**

Hay House Titles of Related Interest

YOU CAN HEAL YOUR LIFE, the movie,
starring Louise Hay & Friends
(available as an online streaming video)
www.hayhouse.com/louise-movie

THE SHIFT, the movie,
starring Dr. Wayne W. Dyer
(available as an online streaming video)
www.hayhouse.com/the-shift-movie

*8 SECRETS TO POWERFUL MANIFESTING:
How to Create the Reality of Your Dreams,* by Mandy Morris

*AURA ALCHEMY: Learn to Sense Energy Fields, Interpret the Color
Spectrum, and Manifest Success,* by Amy Leigh Mercree

*COSMIC CARE: Astrology, Lunar Cycles, and Birth Charts for Self-
Care and Empowerment,* by Valerie Tejeda

*INFINITE RECEIVING: Crack the Code to Conscious Wealth
Creation and Finally Manifest Your Dream Life,* by Suzy Ashworth

All of the above are available at your local bookstore,
or may be ordered by contacting Hay House (see next page).

We hope you enjoyed this Hay House book. If you'd like to receive our online catalog featuring additional information on Hay House books and products, or if you'd like to find out more about the Hay Foundation, please contact:

Hay House LLC, P.O. Box 5100, Carlsbad, CA 92018-5100
(760) 431-7695 or (800) 654-5126
www.hayhouse.com® • www.hayfoundation.org

———

Published in Australia by:
Hay House Australia Publishing Pty Ltd
18/36 Ralph St., Alexandria NSW 2015
Phone: +61 (02) 9669 4299
www.hayhouse.com.au

Published in the United Kingdom by:
Hay House UK Ltd
1st Floor, Crawford Corner,
91–93 Baker Street, London W1U 6QQ
Phone: +44 (0)20 3927 7290
www.hayhouse.co.uk

Published in India by:
Hay House Publishers (India) Pvt Ltd
Muskaan Complex, Plot No. 3,
B-2, Vasant Kunj, New Delhi 110 070
Phone: +91 11 41761620
www.hayhouse.co.in

———

Let Your Soul Grow

Experience life-changing transformation—one video
at a time—with guidance from the world's leading experts.

www.healyourlifeplus.com

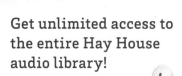